turning toward the
mystery

turning toward the
mystery

A SEEKER'S JOURNEY

stephen levine

HarperSanFrancisco
A Division of HarperCollins*Publishers*

HarperCollins books may be purchased for educational, business, or sales promotional use. For information please write: Special Markets Department, HarperCollins Publishers, Inc., 10 East 53rd Street, New York, NY 10022.

HarperCollins Web site: http://www.harpercollins.com

HarperCollins®, ■®, and HarperSanFrancisco™ are trademarks of HarperCollins Publishers, Inc.

FIRST EDITION

Library of Congress Cataloging-in-Publication Data

Levine, Stephen.
    Turning toward the mystery : a seeker's journey / Stephen Levine
        p.   cm.
    ISBN 0–06–251744–9 (cloth : alk. paper) — ISBN 0–06–251745–7
    1. Levine, Stephen.   2. Spiritual life—Buddhism.   3. Spiritual biography—United States.   I. Title.

    BQ970.L48 A3 2002
    294.3'092—dc21   2001039724

02   03   04   05   06   ❖/RRD   10   9   8   7   6   5   4   3   2   1

contents

contents

contents

PART V: Pilgrim's Progress

acknowledgments

Who does one acknowledge who has not already been mentioned in the story of one's life?

Everyone and everything!

Though a few names and places and the order of certain events have been changed, this is a true story insofar as an imperfect memory and the limitations of egoistic perception will allow.

Great thanks to editor Liz Perle at HarperSanFrancisco, whose heart was the perfect mirror for this rather tricky undertaking.

introduction

an accessible grace

Some call the vast unknown the mystery. Some who sense a perfect order to it call it the Tao (oddly capitalizing it, making a proper noun out of an endless verb, much as we do with "God" or "Buddha" or "I"). Those living in harmony with the earth may refer to it as nature's unfolding or the way of things.

Turning toward the mystery, we explore the unknown. First the investigation of the mystery of ourselves: psychological, to a point, after which it is spiritual. Then an entering into the universal: spiritual, to a point, after which it is indefinable.

Turning inward leads to the uncovering and healing of our small self, our personal myth, the mental construct in which we mistakenly believe our true self is housed.

And as we look deeper for something yet more real, in sudden wordless understandings, levels of awareness are revealed that direct the pilgrim home.

This is the account of a wandering awareness gradually drawn toward the light. The process of a long spiritual practice steadily met by a mysterious grace.

I write about early internal struggles not to add to the self-serving drama of a memoir, but for the benefit of any who might find in my confusion some way out of their own.

After more than forty years of spiritual practice and a gradual awakening from a very deep sleep, I write this book to share the process of an accessible grace.

turning toward the
mystery

PART 1

a full beginning

ONE

breathing in

I was born a hungry ghost.

Ill from a protracted digestive disorder that, after more than two years of the old doctor's insistence on absolutely nothing but mashed bananas and skimmed milk, left me severely malnourished. Pleading for food, I am told, when I smelled dinner being served to the family downstairs. My beleaguered parents, on taking me to a new physician, were told that the problem was no longer the celiac condition, but slow starvation.

I had a pocketful of stolen candy bars by the age of four.

By eight years old I walked nine blocks to and from P.S. #16 with one of two neighbors nearly every day.

Tommy was a friend I had known since I was a toddler. A wistful, obsessive, deeply internalized, oxygen-deprived-at-birth fellow. For years during our walk home he would at times pass on, in an obsessive-compulsive flow, more than I will ever need to know about the fine points of automobile chrome plating. By sixth grade his interest had shifted to the microdesign of various fountain pens. Because he dragged one foot slightly it was a slow walk home. It was a teaching in warmth and patience. It was the path with a heart.

The other fellow, named Hap, lived up to his name—smart, a joker, stimulating playmate, and fellow shoplifter. We had a penchant for stealing war toys and, for some reason, stuffed olives. Ours was the fast, look-over-your-shoulder path home.

My best friend Eric died when we were nine. We used to sit on his front porch two blocks from P.S. #16, watching the cars going by and imagining who we might be when we grew up.

He was the only person I knew with an accent. We laughed a lot. He had an unusual generosity. He would often hand me what I wanted before I mentioned it. He was my favorite playmate.

I learned some time later that he died of "the sickness," probably leukemia, acquired two years earlier when subjected to chemical experimentation in Auschwitz.

Every few weeks my father smelled of vanilla.

He had built up a small household chemical-manufacturing business. Developing, among other products, a line of blueing and ammonia, a remarkably effective vitamin B-12 plant-growth additive, and a chemical stew for the nickel-plating industry that eliminated the need to polish after plating. And, too, imitation vanilla on a bottling line of his own design and construction.

His small factory was in a hundred-year-old brick building in the oldest part of town. On its cellar walls could still be seen the faint remnants of "party painting" from the days when it was a speakeasy run by Legs Diamond.

Two blocks from his factory was a once elegant, now quite dilapidated movie theater that showed mostly westerns and war movies.

At a Saturday matinee western when I was thirteen, an older man sat next to me and offered me some popcorn. He asked if I would I like to go for a ride, even drive his panel truck parked just outside. I pretty much knew what he was up to. Reaching into my jacket pocket to touch the small pistol I had stolen in a burglary, I considered robbing him and taking his truck. I told him I'd be right back after I went to the bathroom.

When I opened the door to the dingy men's room walled in soiled, cracked, and stained tile, I was immediately enveloped in acrid smoke. Bent over the sink a hunched figure was burning a small pile of what I now understand was belladonna, stramonium, inhaled for what must have been a severe asthma attack.

The broken old room full of bitter smoke from what seemed some drug demon hovering in the corner, and me with a loaded pistol, and someone waiting back in the dark for me to rob him, or worse.

My chest burned with fear and belladonna. It was unmistakably hell.

I slipped out the side door into the sunshine.

A few months later I was arrested for carrying that gun. I was surprised by the feeling that somehow it really didn't matter because my life was already over.

At the time I thought a gun was some sort of magical talisman, a symbol of safety and autonomy.

I had not realized yet that a gun was just a second spine. It was going to take me a while.

Ghost though I was, nonetheless I was blessed. Though it would be a very slow revelation, unexpected imperatives about noninjury and the unanticipated sacredness of life arose from a heart I did not even know I had. They were lifelines from the mystery by which I began to pull myself up and out of the primal ooze of my fear and isolation.

The first of two mantras that gravitated into my world came just before I was arrested. In a moment of stress and grace, with the police not far behind, "God Is Love" reached me. It spoke to me from a cro-cheted sampler on the wall behind the kindest adult I had yet met while he held me as I wept trembling in fear.

As my concepts of God have changed over the years, these words have meandered through many levels of meaning. But always love has been as good a word for the Divine as I could imagine.

Love is the emptiness of everything but love.

For as long as I can remember the alternate antics of the wounded child and the investigations of the ageless Universal played through me.

In the beginnings of my secluded cellar laboratory, which my chemist father had mostly provided, these two tendencies were clearly acted out. On the one hand, I experimented making gunpowder pyrotechnics, while, on the other hand, I was carefully constructing an Archimedes' Vertigo to see what was to be found at the hypnotic cen-ter of the spinning concentric circles. A swirling, presumably mind-manifesting vertigo I had drawn meticulously with black crayon on a cardboard circle spun by the small motor from my Erector set. It was constructed to see what horizons lay beyond the brain-spin and simple dizziness of the child's arms-extended twirling. Early heart recalling ancient dervishings perhaps.

Entering high school I was given the second mantra, "*Om Mani Padme Hum*" (a Tibetan mantra, often translated as "O, Thou Jewel in the Lotus Flower"). Shared as the mysterious "heathen mumblings"

heard across the valley by my closest friend, whose family had been Christian missionaries on the border of Tibet in the late '40s. He spoke of seeing the Great Wall as a child.

The mantra became our "inside greeting," part of the mystical code of friendship, repeated thousands of times during our adolescence. We did not know what a mantra was or even that anything was sacred. It did not deepen us, but it did serve as a kind of safety rope between us in our often steep, occasionally dangerous, and slightly criminal rites of passage.

We pronounced it something like, "Oh, Manny pad me hum," often flashing our palm for a reciprocal play slap when "pad me" was said. Ironically, even though it was done with all the wrong intentions except for our contract of trust, it did have a connecting energy that remains to this day. It still represents at the very least courage and brotherhood.

In the Tibetan monastery the jewel referred to in the lotus flower may be the dharma (the teachings) or the essence of Being, but to us the jewel was what was referred to on the street as "heart." *Om Mani Padme Hum* will always remind me of that mix of loyalty and strength of intention, and of all the "heart" it takes to make it to the center of the lotus.

Repeated so often between teenage riotings with the gang, it never seemed of any evident spiritual avail. There are those who would say there might have been merit or benefit accumulated by even our mindless repetition, but I would strongly differ. In reciting a mantra, as in all spiritual practice, indeed as in the very basis of karma (life momentum), it is the intention that does all the work.

Despite our youthful heresy and frivolity accompanying its repetition, I apparently did not ruin it for myself. Ironically, years later Rudi, my first teacher, gave it to me as my first mantra, saying it might help in approaching the towering cathedral doors at the center of the chest. The mantra kept my smallness steady in the face of the enormity.

Decades later, during a conference, standing and holding hands with His Holiness the Dalai Lama, I recalled that lotus song, that "mantra with a heart" that had accompanied me for so long through so many incarnations in this lifetime. *Om Mani Padme Hum* and his eternal smile reached all the way across the valley. Sitting at the foot of the Great Wall taking tea and mantra, youthful, ready to climb. Dreaming in the shadows, dreaming in the sun.

Indeed, the distance between heart and mind was oddly evident even in rough youth. Though I had an interest in science and music not widely shared by the group, I was happily a member of a rather dynamic teenage collective. We were not a gang by today's standards. Indeed, we were more of a territorial car club.

Though on rare occasion we "rumbled," I was not much of a fighter. Oddly, though I still had a pistol stashed away as a talisman against my stashed-away fears, for some reason profoundly mysterious to me at the time, even in a street fight I had an innate imperative not to hurt another. I would, surprising myself, be cautious not to injure.

On one occasion, I let go of a fellow I was concerned I might hurt when he was down. He was much bigger than I, and it would have been something of a triumph to have overcome him. But I could not strike the blow that would have made him "cry uncle." And he, with a much different sense of the appropriate, got up and beat me senseless.

An almost Norman Rockwell–like image remains from those days of the six-foot two-inch, two-hundred-plus-pound Carmina, who could beat most of us arm wrestling, angry she could not come along as we departed for the appointed brawl, her arms covered from wrist to biceps with all our wristwatches left for safekeeping.

Driving back from one of these teachings in nonviolence, flanked by comrades in arms, the adrenaline metabolized, we found ourselves slipping into a rather fatalistic conversation. Johnny K., then twenty-two, said he wouldn't live to be twenty-five. I, seventeen and very much in the dark spirit of the moment, said I wouldn't live to see twenty-one. Mark, driving his newly completed street drag-racing coup, said he'd beat us both.

Within two years both of them had been killed in separate crashes.

Arrested four times before I was nineteen, I knew something had to change or I too would lose my life.

TWO

the will toward mystery

We have a will toward mystery, a yearning, greater even than our will to live. And lucky, too, because our will to live, our grasping at life, is killing us.

The will toward mystery is our homesickness for God.

The will to live is our fear of death, our clinging to pleasure, our dread of not becoming. The will to live often mistakes itself for the mind and body. It is part of what enlightenment frees us from.

The will to live keeps us hard-bellied, holding each breath, backed into a corner, three-quarters blind. Bartering the full perspective for the illusion of safety.

Though the absence, or suppression, of the will to live can unquestionably cause a kind of lifelessness and melancholy, its limited definition of living may do the same.

But the presence of what is called the Great Desire, the will toward mystery, the longing for deeper knowing, the draw toward the sacred heart, redefines life. A gradual upwelling of the still small voice within is heard. And sudden wordless understandings arise that nearly take our breath away.

There is a grace approaching that we shun as much as death. It is the completion of our birth, the self-actualization that is the goal of so much psychological and spiritual endeavor.

It does not come in time, but in timelessness, when the mind sinks into the heart, when thoughts begin to transform from blame to acceptance and appreciation, and even praise. And we remember who we really are.

It is an insistent grace that draws us to the edge and beckons us to surrender safe territory and enter our enormity.

THREE

i and I and all that jazz

At eighteen, after a rhythmical summer, I went off to the academically weak but musically strong University of Miami. Having taken up my instrument, drums, much later than most of my musical contemporaries, I was a would-be jazz musician. I was learning from everybody.

After listening as a child in my morning bed to the robins in the tree outside my window, my first deep reflections were on sound. Music was my first deep connection with a sense of being, jazz my first journey to the other side of the brain. It called the song out of me. And listening to it even now seems to draw the heart toward the center of the sound.

In those initiatory college days in the jazz clubs of Miami, we used to sit in and "jam with the big boys." A small circle of young musicians educated by the many visiting musicians who joked that they "came down to clean up." But we were all a bit too close to Jamaica and old Cuba for that.

In the summer before my sophomore year my mother took me across state lines to hear jazz.

She wanted to know something of my world before I disappeared completely into it. We went to several jazz concerts. Many times we drove from Albany over the perfect New England scenic route of the Old Post Road toward Tanglewood and the Lenox Music Barn. We sat speechless together as such national treasures as the Modern Jazz Quartet thrilled us and took us to places we had never shared.

And I heard the other day that Milt Jackson, the MJQ's contemplative vibraphonist, known affectionately as Bags (for the soft satchels under his eyes), just died. And I think somewhere in paradise (whether within me or within her) my mother is tapping her proper toe in quiet shoes, and Bags can't keep from smiling.

In the late '50s in jazz Miami I made the acquaintance of many musicians influenced by the Rastafari faith who sometimes lyrically referred to themselves as what I imagine would be written "i and I." They included themselves and the Divine in the same breath.

It was an early initiation into an intimacy with God that I would not discover again until decades later when I read the God-drunken poetry of Kabir and felt the perfect circles traced by Rumi on the supplicant's heart.

My heart literally ached for such devotional connection. Their love of the Beloved made those first meditations between notes lush with the sacred. It was the introduction of self to Self.

I and I, the ever present closeness of the sacred. God and We made of each other's boundless likeness.

Indeed, "i and I" displays the two levels of healing that our birth calls forth. The first is of the mind recognizing itself, awareness of awareness, self-discovery; the investigation of small self. The second is of the heart recognizing first the world, then the Universe. The discovery of the most of us, the exploration of Big Self.

When I speak of the self (uncapitalized), I am referring to the personal self. When I use the term Self (capitalized), I am speaking of the great Self, the Divine, the Godhead, the essence of Being.

In Buddhism these different levels of consciousness referred to as small self and Big Self are often seen as small or little mind and Big Mind.

The experiences of the boundless spaciousness at our center, which once experienced might be called Big Self in Hinduism or the Jesus connection, might in Buddhism's existential view be verbalized as no-self.

Indeed, "i and I" to the Buddhist might seem to be "double trouble," while to the devotional temperament it might represent the singular delight of the union of the personal and the universal.

To one worldview "i and I" may appear as the duality that separates us from the source of consciousness. While to another it is the essential relationship with the Divine, the ultimate duality that, piercing "the cloud of unknowing," the space between the sacred and the profane, culminates in absolute Oneness.

Big Self and no-self only differ to the small self. All traditions melt into the will toward mystery, the longing. Each seeks liberation from suffering and a greater sense of presence.

And as I learned so slowly beyond the smoke and chatter of the jazz clubs:

It is easier to say i and I than to be it.
Even when the music is like water,
even when the air is fresh with His breath,
even when the song never ends,
it is easier said than done and done.
But sometimes i and I disappear into no edges
    by which to be defined—

just the embrace
of proton and neutron, hydrogen and oxygen,
sperm and egg, sacred and supplicant.
And the ease of simply being
like Kabir's Beloved to be found "in the breath within the breath."
But as you and I well know, i and I is One.

FOUR

narcissus's heart

Shut away alone in an upstairs room in those early years and feeling sorry for yourself tends to make one rather narcissistic. The whole world shrinks to the size of your pain, a very tight fit. Only you alone are left to protect yourself and the world from catching fire. When you are excluded from the family, you have to create your own religion.

With the theology of ego-as-center-of-the-universe numbing my pain, I became indifferent to the pain of others. With my heart so often like a stone, I acted in such a hurtful manner that considerable apology is due.

When I came to see from a place other than that pained consciousness, I knew that somehow I had to heal this narcissistic pain and complete my birth. I had to find out who I was beneath all the fear and confusion, to heal the mind into the heart, to find peace.

At times in meditation, that confused child that I was would crawl into my arms and tremble with feelings of abandonment, until meditation floated away the fear that no one could love him.

Indeed, that child might have stayed submerged in a kind of emaciated self-pity if I had not cared so much for him, nurtured him, and begun slowly to unwrap his cocoon.

Releasing a child's grief from its bindings is a work of self-mercy so tender and subtle it purifies the air you and your loved ones breathe. But we need to be very mindful, because we are so attached to our suffering. It makes up a large part of our identity. Narcissus often uses pain to define, even outline, the image he finds reflected on the murky surface of the mind.

Reading the Upanishads and the biographies of Krishnamurti and Gandhi, I came to feel that liberation might be possible after all.

At nineteen I left college to have an operation to remove two herniated disks from my lower lumbar region.

When I read that in Eastern belief systems there is thought to be a powerful wisdom energy called *kundalini*, represented as a mystical serpent coiled at the base of the spine, I mused even then that my physical condition might have resulted from a blocking of that legendary *kundalini*.

At twenty, with already so much done and undone, with time clearly waiting in ambush, I met Buddha in a bus station. From a rack of loosely browsed paperbacks, the Buddha's countenance emerged luminous from A. E. Burt's *The Compassionate Buddha*. In his Four Noble Truths the Buddha told me I wasn't the only one suffering. He said the pain came from the emotional exhaustion of grasping at the ever changing, even illusory, nature of things. He said there was a way out. He offered a path toward clarity and kindness.

And the mind turned intuitively toward the mystery. The slow healing began as the heart recognized that the understanding arising from my readings was just the beginning. In fleeting moments of quiet, the benefits of stillness became quite evident. It was time to begin the actual practice of freeing myself from suffering.

After the back operation, I returned to Miami and rented a sparsely converted two-car garage to begin what I hoped and expected would be an extended period of secluded meditation.

The only problem with what came to be called Buddha's Garage was that I did not know how to meditate. But I did have some idea of what an ascetic lifestyle might be. I took a vow to step back from pleasure. I sat respectfully before a plaster dime-store Buddha and wished I was at peace.

But my earliest misreadings of Buddhism were reinforcing a Judeo-Christian penchant for self-negation. In the '50s all I could find after *The Compassionate Buddha* caught my eye at the bus station was the very professorial D. T. Suzuki, who is as thickly intellectual as a Zen Master gets.

I was getting all the superstition and philosophy, but none of the meditation instruction on how not to get ensnarled by such idealized thinking.

I became confused about what to do with desire. Uncertain how to resolve the increasing confusion between what seemed like natural drives and the much-touted, religiously approved state of desirelessness.

Conflicted by the notion that desire was to be avoided while at the same time being exhorted to want myself and the world to be different, I was in two.

Words like "renunciation" spun through my libidinous twenty-year-old mind and found me profoundly unworthy of Buddha's blessing. How could I ever extirpate myself from this morass of wanting? How much of myself would I have to kill?

How could I have been born so far from God?

FIVE

learning to read and write the mystery

Retreating from Buddha's Garage in dazed dismay and with a sense of deep self-doubt by the time I was twenty-one, I was so confounded by the suffering within and around me I wanted out.

My first piece of writing was a suicide-optional note. It was the word "why?" typed dozens of times. At first I just wrote "why?" repeatedly, then noticed I had the option of capitalizing the first letter of "Why," and after a few "Why?"s it occurred to me that I could capitalize any letter . . . and so I did. I wrote "wHy?" "whY?" "WhY?" and then I noticed there was a double-color ribbon in the typewriter and I could alternate red letters with black, or do them any way I wanted! And by the end of this very free-flowing, actually very exciting creativity much had changed. The note went from the left to the right brain, from artifact to art, and what had been written became "a piece of writing."

The ordinary mind as it is released from its narrow confines into the opening heart makes the most beautiful sounds. Music and poetry rise light as bell tones.

Writing offered me a new life, and the investigation of the mystery within and around me made it worth living. These words spontaneously arising, so pained at times, so lovely at others, began slowly to speak themselves, began to rhapsodize about the qualities of the heart.

Even decades after its beginnings, getting out of the way of the mind and putting forth the heart, which is writing at its best, continues to beckon the healing I took birth for, the completion. To call the mind into the heart reminds me to tell the truth and meditate a bit more on what I dare call truth.

The note came in very handy a few weeks later when, the depression remaining, I wanted quick entrée into the New York State Psychiatric Institute. I thought it was time to fix my mind before it got any darker and give my heart a chance.

But even in the institution the mystery found me. Sensing I had to get beneath my anger and fear, I sought a deeper way. From sources that are still unclear, two very powerful guidebooks for the journey appeared and became my sane companions. My two wisdom teachers were Sivananda's *Meditation* and the masterful Vivekananda's *Raja Yoga*. Two of the most respected spiritual masters of their period. And for the first time, more than just philosophy or spiritual testimony, actual methods of centering the mind and freeing the heart became part of the inner equation. Through Vivekananda, who became so widely respected for his teachings in this country at the turn of the century, I received the yogic principles of the great spiritual master Patanjali for uniting with the Absolute, connecting me with the breath and inviting a new relationship to my pain by displaying what lay beyond it. Displaying that as we enter the breath and let go of who we think we are, we become more than we ever imagined. That no matter how closed the mind or frightened the heart, the mystery is always at play. That liberation is always available. That remarkable openings can occur when the great sigh of letting go, of sinking through level after level of fear and holding, reaches the heart. And from Sivananda strong encouragement to turn toward an intensity of practice like that found in India.

Even on the tenth floor of a mental institution in the midst of New York City, the mystery reminded me of my deeper nature. Lying very still on my bed, I found my breath. Within the breath was a passageway to the heart I had long been seeking. As I attempted to unleash the yogic energy of the breath, the interweaving cooing of the pigeons on the ledge just outside my window became indistinguishable from the subtle intonations within the breath. My breath and the earth's breath in perfect harmony, reconnecting me with the planet and the animal spirits thereon, which were becoming my first deep muse. As I was lying there, poetry began spontaneously to recite itself in my expanding mind. Each day thereafter a poem arose in praise of the enormity into which I found I fit so perfectly.

I did not know how I had lost that primal connection with the natural mystery. But I knew I was being drawn in the right direction. Reconnecting with the earth even on the Upper West Side of Manhattan was clearly demonstrated on the evening of the first snow. A dozen of us gathered around the broad rec-room window watching the snow accumulate on the street below. Snowflakes drifted illuminated under the overhanging streetlights. Nurses and patients stood rapt together in silent admiration for the stunning beauty of the unbroken snow.

After ten minutes, a single car passing by tore the shimmering canvas, ripping two long lizard tracks in the perfect snow. The analogy with the loss of innocence too obvious to overlook. A few sobbing in the dark rec room.

Such experiences of interbeing—that sense of deep, even profound, interconnectedness that often causes a feeling of oneness to arise—increase confidence in the possibility of a true and deep healing.

This draw toward our natural common center and the poetry that praises it offered considerable insight into the healing of the mind and

the opening of the heart as something one must do for oneself, no matter the guidance. "The work to be done, the grace we are!" whispers
the inner chorus.

Though I had signed myself into the institution because I thought
they fixed minds, I found they didn't do that sort of thing. They dealt
mostly with the content, which can be helpful. And sometimes with
the patterns, which can be releasing. But rarely with the process,
which can be healing. And never with the ground of being, the awareness, the presence, it's all floating in, which can be transformative.

Having exchanged my Miami meditation garage for a few months
in the fluorescent-lit halls of the New York Psychiatric Institute, I
signed myself out into a brand-new world. Those first poems in my
winter pocket; each line repairing the broken snow.

(The mystery loves the cyclical nature of coincidence, and twenty
years after leaving the New York Psychiatric Institute, I acted as something of an advisor on the gravely ill children's floor at Babies Hospital
of the same Columbia-Presbyterian Medical Center.

And ten years after that, because I had written about Vivekananda's
bright, devoted insight and its effect on me, I was invited to India as
a guest speaker at the massive celebration of the anniversary of
Vivekananda's groundbreaking speech at the 1893 World's Parliament
of Religions in Chicago.)

Returning to a brave new world, I took the A train the length of
the island and settled in Greenwich Village, where I connected immediately with the jazz-loving, hard-traveling, spirit-leaning, up-all-night
artist community.

Monk was at the Five Spot. Miles was uptown at Birdland. Danny
Proper was starting to read with Mingus. Allen Ginsberg was cantoring
with his harmonium. Poetry and jazz were melding.

Employed in coffee shops as a cook or waiter, I got my fill of eight hours a day of Bach harpsichord and Segovia from the hourly repeated tape loop. Reading poetry at various loft gatherings and working as a short-order cook at the Gaslight on MacDougal Street, I was asked to coordinate what became the long-standing, semiliterate Sunday "Poetry of the Beat Generation" readings. It was a rich and wild "bouillabaisse of poetry," as one unfortunate poet put it.

It was composed of the best and most hopeful of the time, ranging from Diane DiPrima, Gregory Corso, Taylor Mead, John Brent, Peter Zimmels, Hugh Romney (not quite yet Wavy Gravy), and Ray Bremser to wild-eyed poets who said they had to whistle the first few lines because the words hadn't come to them yet.

On four consecutive Thursdays nights I shared an octopus with the noted poet W. H. Auden in his St. Marks Street flat directly across from my favorite jazz club, in which Lord Buckley made his holy row, as did Art Blakey and the Jazz Messengers, and Horace Silver and his posse.

Chester, Auden's longtime companion, had originally invited me to supper to meet Auden and often generously acted as my interpreter. When I asked Auden what he thought of Antonin Artaud's influence on the new—sometimes called "beat"—poetry, he said it was "bathroom reading." When I later showed him my work, he frowned and said, "Everyone below 14th Street thinks they're a poet!" Just the encouragement a young poet needed! A few days later I recounted the conversation to Ray Bremser; the next day he and Kerouac knocked on Auden's door and "half pretended to throttle him."

Those first poems dedicated to suffering and hopeful of release were published in 1959 as *A Resonance of Hope*, which says at one point, "I still have no answer to me," and ends with the line, "And there shall be Dust." But clearly, though there was poetry and spirit in my life, before the ends could come together to form a perfect circle, some less wholesome inclinations and intentions had to play themselves out, old momentums had yet to be resolved, suffering had yet to meet its grace.

A year after moving to the Village I was married. My first wife and I were perfectly suited, she an escapee from a difficult realm, and I still with considerable underlying anger and anxious for more experience. Together we dabbled in heroin.

Her Jamaican stepfather was Tom Tear, the antihero in *Cain's Book*, Alex Trocchi's grim tale of addiction. Brought into the fold, I was invited for "tea and poppies" by Trocchi, a highly regarded literary figure and notorious addict in England.

The gods of the beat generation, musically and poetically, were often an odd improvisational mixture of a sometimes nihilistic, somewhat gaudy Buddha and a generous, even inspiring Morpheus. A popular combo at the time for dharma bums and the subterranean poetic society of "angel-headed hipsters."

Soon I was injecting small quantities intramuscularly for gradual absorption, producing what amounted to opium dreams. I had no "tracks" on my arms. But my gluteus looked like a pincushion.

Alex and I worked well together, and he asked me to help with the completion of a long overdue anthology called *Writers in Revolt*. Alex, Dick Seaver, the Grove Press editor of the seminal avant-garde *Evergreen Review*, and Terry Southern, author of *Candy* and soon-to-be scriptwriter of the film *Dr. Strangelove*, had been compiling the anthology for quite a while and just wanted to finish it up.

When the anthology was completed, Terry, thinking I should get above 14th Street, approached the publisher of the anthology and, praising my work, suggested he hire me. Which he did.

I worked for more than a year as an editor for that New York publisher, during which time the spiral of coincidence offered a most remarkable healing.

For many years I was filled with rage and sadness when I thought of what had been done to my childhood friend Eric.

Almost fifteen years after his death, into my editorial office with a manuscript under her arm came the surviving wife of a leading Polish pathologist who was forced, his wife and child held hostage, to assist Dr. Mengele in his horrific experimentation at Auschwitz. Dr. Nysili, a man of immense compassion, died of what seems a broken heart soon after he and his family were liberated from the death camps.

There were times working with this drained, nearly translucent woman on the preparation of her manuscript, *Auschwitz*, when I wondered whether her husband might have known Eric. If, indeed, he might have held five-year-old Eric's trembling arm a little lighter, even recited a prayer, when he reluctantly administered the caustic injections that eventually broke Eric's body.

Though of course there was no way of asking or answering such a question, sometimes I would see them together. The doctor with his arm around all the children. And his never ending tears. And the children pulling at his coat, reminding him of how beautiful even a broken heart can be.

After two years my wife and I, never having deeply bonded perhaps because we were both hiding so far inside ourselves we never reached across the chasm, parted very amicably when she went off traveling and I took my turn in prison. She, of considerable intelligence and inner strength, in the next years transformed herself from high-school dropout to a Ph.D. and is at present head of her department in a major university. I, having been arrested for drug possession, left my editorial desk behind and followed the mystery to the Rikers Island Penitentiary.

karma savings and loan

Soon after I was incarcerated, I began tunneling my way to freedom. I began once again to meditate. I dreamed of a universe within that was greater than any in which I found myself imprisoned in steel and body and mind.

Surrendering one tenuous breath after another, I saw through my bars. In each breath there was room to grow and all I needed to get by the pain, which forgets.

Even in jail the mystery offered precious opportunity.

While spending a few moments "on the island," I edited the prison newspaper. The prison newspaper was next to the art shop. It was quite common for inmates to ask the art shop to silk-screen a birthday card for a wife or child. And for the inmate to then sneak next door and, giving me a few pertinent facts, request a quick poem, a brief salutation, or a something-but-do-it-quick-before-the-guard-comes. It was training in the Zen of poetry. They were "first thought, best thought" poems. My sobriquet became "quick poet."

The books that directed me and were my companions on this segment of the journey were Ezra Pound's *Confucian Odes*, Kerouac's

Mexico City Blues, and the master guide to conscious navigation, the *Tao Te Ching.*

The *Rikers Review* turned out to be a surprisingly good publication: our music page was compiled by a *DownBeat* jazz poll winner; our chess page (a main occupation in jail; may I never play another game of chess again!) was by a fellow well on his way to becoming a grand master. The inmate writings ranged from supplications to the Divine to epic poems of horrid childhood battles won and lost against the tenement rats.

And Unlucky Tom, who helped run the printing press and was arrested again the day after he was released: prosecuted, sentenced, and returned to prison within a week of being paroled. Who twenty years later called to say he was dying of cancer, could we spend some time together. Late-Blessed Tom, whose death was so much better than his life.

One of the staff on the paper was a friend from the Village, arrested for his attempt at one of the first LSD laboratories in 1961. A pale, soft-spoken, bespectacled scientist who had gotten in over his head in more ways than one. "I got arrested by mistake!" he said.

There had been a knock on his third-floor steel tenement door one Saturday afternoon. When he asked who was it, the reply was, "Police!" And he panicked and threw his lab out the window. Lots of glassware and two fishing-tackle boxes full of chemicals, hardware, pot, pills, and paraphernalia made quite a racket as they crashed to the sidewalk below. Barely missing the patrolman stationed on the front stoop, as they searched for the person who had burglarized a downstairs apartment—the reason they had knocked on his door in the first place, simply seeking information. And the lab-hazed, overamped denizens behind the steel door all went to jail.

He was not at all what generally might be considered a "criminal type." Noticeably out of place in the prison, he was quite vulnerable and was about to be "taken" by an older, much stronger inmate. Seeing no alternative, I had to step in and say, "He's mine!" to stop a problem my friend was about to be unable to solve. My friend was as astonished as I was. But because I had once done an "instant poem" for the would-be attacker's son's birthday card, he backed off.

I could hardly believe I said something so against my prejudices and negative conditioning. I, who so narrow of mind and thoroughly homophobic when a young teen, reading Walt Whitman almost turned away wondering, "This guy couldn't be! Could he?" A deep bow to master Whitman and the life teachings that take us beyond our personal edge into participation in the whole.

Just before I was released, Terry Southern, about to head west to create his groundbreaking film, then acting as temporary poetry editor for the *Paris Review*, wrote to say they intended to publish two of my poems in a forthcoming issue. And, scrambling my delight, added, "But poetry is too easy." He was right it was far too soon to settle, in the face of the hard work yet to be done.

On the ferry to freedom, watching the prison recede and the city approach, I knew that as the poetry that blossomed on Ward B had to be taken to fertile ground, so too the tender roots of the meditation practice developing on Cellblock C would need warmth and nourishment to come to fruition.

Though I knew I needed to break the hard-drug cycle in order to establish a clear-minded spiritual practice, I felt something still lingering in my gut.

"After all, even Jesus had an Antichrist!" mumbled the still hungry ghost longing to be filled.

Having gradually renewed use six months after I was released, I was soon well over my edge. On parole, my sometimes lover pregnant, seeking a then illegal abortion, her father an angry FBI agent threatening to return me to prison.

Teetering on the brink, with my toes curled over the edge, I didn't like the view. I knew better.

When the two years of parole were completed in 1964, I decided it was time to change worlds and go to Mexico "kicking" (dropping whatever habituation had accumulated) as I drove.

But it was going to be a while before teachings such as the Buddha's sank deep enough to affect romanticized self-destructive behavior. Before the dharma became more than a periodic endeavor.

Expecting to arrive clean in sunny Mexico City, only to pull into the infamous old Hotel Nunca near the Zocolo just as a "new shipment" arrived.

Hanging out with an ex–call girl from Chicago who was studying native weaving, I wrote poetry during the day and shot heroin with a gang of Mexican pickpockets at night. The fever flickering.

Even the addiction I cultivated under that dull yellow bulb above my favorite tattered couch on the "shooting balcony" could not obscure the longing for wholeness that continued to insinuate itself into my shadowy corner.

One night, sick-addicted on my way to get dosed and disappear into my couch, I became enraged at a long stoplight in Mexico City. Pounding on the steering wheel, nauseous and drenched in sweat, I knew I had to do something right then or I would be sick the rest of my life. It was agonizingly clear that heroin could kill the pain, but not the suffering. And that even such understandings were not enough to open the closed fist of addiction.

I knew I wanted God and clarity more than anything. Weeping, I pulled off the road and stayed there soaked in perspiration and tears with my head in my hands for perhaps an hour. A sweet voice repeated slowly and without the nervous urgency of the body, "You have to want something more than this to be free of it. You must choose between God and heroin!" And it was over! And so it has been ever since.

It takes a big desire to dislodge addiction. Something you want more than dreaming a life away. Ramakrishna speaks of using a bigger thorn to pick out a smaller one. In the world of form, as Carl Jung pointed out to the founders of Alcoholics Anonymous, God, "a higher power," is often the most skillful thorn.

One of the great difficulties drugs create is that, for some, the first time they use drugs may be the first time in their life they feel completely satisfied. Which leads to the morbid dissatisfaction we call addiction, as they attempt for the rest of their lives to recapture that moment of satisfaction.

Indeed, meditators too sometimes suffer from a considerable "letdown" after their first deeply satisfying insight experience. But for meditators the tools to deal with varying states of mind are well established, whereas for drug users their only tool intensifies suffering the more they attempt to relieve it. I had a friend with a severe stutter who during his first use of heroin was able to speak without difficulty. He told me the next day he was already addicted for life. He died of an overdose a few years later.

After nine reckless months, having completed the cycle, the choice made at the stoplight, once again kicking as I drove, I headed north to retrieve my soul.

The mystery loves to test the righteous, so even though I have not "used" in thirty-five years, I walk lightly when I say, particularly with an exclamation mark, "It was over!" I have had at times almost unlimited access to drugs such as morphine at the bedsides of the dying. And over the years I have flushed hundreds of doses down the toilet in cleaning up after a death. Not tempted.

As I attended to the mystery's attempted interventions and the constant teachings from the heart both as karma (momentum, perhaps in the form of a familiar pain) and dharma (the profound relief of rediscovered spaciousness), clarity and forgiveness began gradually to appear.

Approaching the truth is always dependent on our intention and willingness to go farther, to trust the sense of connectedness experienced as we are drawn into the mystery of ourselves.

Angels train in hell for the ineffable compassion of heaven.

Forty years ago, I meditated most of the day in my cell. It was a happy birthday.

Something gentler than before embraced my long-disrespected heart and encouraged that fist long cramped clamped around it to open. Slowly, painfully peeling back one difficult holding after another to eventually reveal the spaciousness of the natural open heart.

This "something gentler" displayed again and again that, when the fist was closed, all I had in there was me. But when it opened I had room for it all, for the healing to be done.

The mystery whispered to that in me which feared it might never *really* open into its heart. It said to remember that Buddha spoke of the ironically intense effort it takes to become effortless, of liberation taking *eons*, and suggested, like the great Tibetan saint Milarepa, to the overeager, prone-to-judgment-mind, to "hasten slowly." Or as Zen Master Sueng Sahn would later say, "Just go straight!"

May all beings be free from suffering. May all beings be at peace.

in the space between births

SEVEN

a short visit in god

On the way to San Francisco, I rented a cottage by the Pacific Ocean for a few weeks of purification and reflection on my relationship with the Divine, to powwow with God before the next leg of the journey.

When I was a child, God was who I prayed to. God was fear, the father, not divine. Then I escaped from God, and in an adolescent ear Nietzsche intoned that there was no God after all, only the Furies and the broken heart. God was dead, and only I was alive.

But as I grew older, no matter how I tried I could not keep God dead. He changed guises from the power above to the power within.

Because I learned early on that "God Is Love" in the midst of turmoil, I on occasion use these words interchangeably. I do not mean to imply a Person or Personage, Judge or Architect. I simply mean that level of mind we call heart when cultivated to exclude nothing. Or its revealed nature in the effortless flow of level after level of creation. But whatever we name the unnamable, it belongs to no one and everyone belongs to It.

Now having come to what seemed, on so many levels, a midpoint between destinations, sitting on the beach reading Buddhist scriptures, it seemed to me that the surrender of the devotional heart was committed to precisely the same process as the letting go inspired by the Buddha mind as it becomes all heart, opening into the mystery.

In a gradually deepening stillness not cluttered by drugs or small talk or appointments, I sat for hours at the edge of the continent looking out to sea. Over the next three weeks, each day I felt quite remarkably as if another weight had been lifted and the sense of lightness increased. Gradually a delightful sense of simply being grew. I was happy in a very different way than I could remember being before.

I was later told that sometimes when people turn wholly toward a spiritual practice and make it part of their daily existence, a kind of "karmic catch-up," a brief period of unusual clarity and open-heartedness, can occur that brings one up to speed. Perhaps to where that practice may have left off in a previous incarnation, or just the given grace of what might be available in that practice.

In a very gradual manner, like the paint on an old canvas wearing thinner each day, the original drawing began to show through, and the sacred could be seen peeking through everything. Everything was a metaphor for God. Even God was a metaphor for God.

God was in the trees and pebbles, in the earth and in the sky and in my eyes.

I was absorbed into the ground of being. I could not tell where God ended and I began. My heart quickened with rapture. God was all that was real and I was just an illusion.

Before I left for San Francisco I wrote myself a note:

In timelessness the gods convene
to become molecules and memories
there is only One of which all else is composed
we are consciousness
in all its unconscious forms . . .

Buddha said it takes eons to be wholly born, for this purification to drop the veils, defeat the hindrances, enter deeper the truth.

EIGHT

opening the lotus, levels of purification

I walked through half my life as if it were a fever dream, barely touch-ing the ground. My eyes half open, my heart half closed. Not half knowing who I was, I watched the ghost of me drift from room to room, through friends and lovers, never quite as real as advertised.

Not saying half of what I meant I dreamt myself from birth to birth seeking some true self until the fever broke and the heart could not endure a moment longer.

And the rest of me awakened in the dream, summoned by the vast-ness to unrealized realms of being.

Born into a more authentic life, not half caring for anything but love.

Healing is a clearing of the path ahead for what used to be called *purification* before Freud and those frightening images of hell projected from so many ancient holy books made us even more frightened and distrusting of ourselves. Purification does not deal in heinous sin or colorful fetish, but simply in letting something more merciful than frightened judgment embrace whatever we fear is impure, whatever remains yet unloved. Some refer to this process as "opening the lotus," because the lotus must rise above often dark and fetid waters before it can come to bloom.

Indeed, in this process I had to remind myself more than once not to think in terms of perfection, but instead of liberation. Watching how feelings of imperfection were drawn toward the "perfection" of the religious ideal (which gives rise to so much judgment and so many holy wars), rather than the liberation of the spirit from such conceptual encumbrances.

Everyone is just trying to get born before they die.

There are ten thousand stepping-stones on the path of healing. They float like galaxies in the mind. Each takes us one step farther into the mystery. None tells us what's next. We honor the mystery with trust in the process.

We are mesmerized by our wounds and unfulfilled desires. We find it difficult to define ourselves without them. They are among the first often-repeated confidences we share.

We will not let go of fear and hatred, no matter how badly they make us feel, because we just don't believe we could "be ourselves" without them. We identify so with our suffering that it is difficult for us to imagine who we would be without it.

LETTING GO

Letting go of our suffering is the hardest work we will ever do, and among the most fruitful and gratifying.

To let go of the pain that had become so familiar it had become endemic to my identity was to recognize how often I had volunteered for hell.

Profoundly dissatisfied as a youth who early saw the world as greatly lacking, I imagined I was one of those it is rumored were born against their will.

Something between empathy and self-pity resonated with the stories I heard of those who, having died into what seemed the most perfect of an afterlife, were advised it was not their time and had to return to their pain-filled, desire-driven, fragile human body.

It is said this wearying sense of unwilling participation in our lives, this feeling of reluctant presence in so many, accounts for the expanding interest in spiritual matters in our society as well as, ironically, for the increase in criminal behavior.

That is why some in their spiritual cycle need to be more wary than most of a tendency toward self-negation. And some in addictive orbits are closer to the *longing* than they will ever know, until they recognize the muffled voices of their hearts.

RENUNCIATION

When in Buddha's Garage I was confused by terms such as *renunciation*. I thought it meant giving up life. Ironically, it was not until I began giving over to service that I came to a different realization. In the alchemical yoga that turns the heart from muscle to light, I discovered that renunciation actually meant doing all you can as well as you can and then letting go of attachment to results, to the fruits of your labors. Renunciation meant trusting the process.

It took a while before I could see beyond the early conditioning that desire and, by inference, pleasure were unwholesome.

My relationship to desire changed with the metamorphosis of my interrelationship with the sacred. Some spiritual adepts, in fact, suggest it is the Great Desire, the will toward mystery, the deep longing for truth, that does all the work.

As I investigated the mechanics of desire, it became clear that desire was not "bad," just *painful*. That desire was a feeling of "not having." A sense of deprivation, of the moment being insufficient, disappointing. The more we want food, love, sex, courage, the greater the feeling of not having them. I saw desire as an undulating nausea in the pit of the hungry ghost's swollen belly.

The goal of desire is that momentary satisfaction when the object of desire is at hand. That satisfaction is a glimpse beyond the desire-agitated mind when desire is momentarily absent, an evanescent peek at the Great Satisfaction. Pleasure is the absence of desire.

And a moment later that object of desire, rather than being the source of satisfaction, stirs vacillating dissatisfaction as attachment to that object, and to satisfaction itself, closes about it and attempts to protect it from decay and change.

A feeling of not-enoughness precedes that instant of happy acquirement. Fear of loss follows it.

The perfection of desire is to go directly to the Great Satisfaction, the sense of completion and ultimate fulfillment at the center of the heart. It cuts out the middleman of lesser desires. The process of perfecting desire opting for a peace and mindfulness that is no longer blocked by fitful wanting.

To recognize the inherent satisfaction just beyond desire is to take the heart's enormous longing for peace as a guide and make that the centerpiece of our will toward mystery.

Mindfulness and mercy for the dry mouth of desire take all those others affected by our tastes a bit more into consideration. The exploration of desire does not lead to an increase in judgment, but to mercy for the angst of our birth. It cultivates compassion, calming that old urgency and anxiety "to get and become" with the support of kindness and patience.

The heart becomes restored when we surrender our pain and begin to release the grasping that turns the open palm to a closed fist.

When the heart peels back those once supple fingers that have gradually become frozen into a fist around its fears and attachments, it is at first surprisingly painful to open that cramped closedness. But it is, as the teachers say, "the pain that ends pain."

When the mind sinks into the heart, the common ordinary grief that misdirects and limits us daily begins to let go of its holding, and a lifelong tension in the belly is noticed to be softening. The armoring melts to plowshares, and peace at last becomes possible.

There are Herculean labors of love to be accomplished in order to break free of the ordinarily lost, small and grieving mind.

As our personal pain eventually gets our attention, we awaken to the universal pain as well and gradually begin to participate in the hurt and healing of all sentient beings.

Slowly we begin sending compassion into our frightened Narcissus. How long will it take to bring our Narcissus off the cross?

NINE

ordinary mind

Thirty years ago, sitting in the No Name Bar in Sausalito with two long-time acquaintances, one a San Francisco poet, the other a member of a local motorcycle gang, the biker asked, "Who was the most rational person ever to have lived?" Without much reflection I said Lao Tzu. They both frowned, shook their heads, and in unison said, "Hitler!" Victims of a tragic logic, I thought, and bowed out of the conversation.

Within a few years one had committed suicide and the other had been shot in the head during a fight.

Although I disagreed at the time, they were in a way correct. The "rational" mind is completely amoral. Offer it a problem, no matter how irrational, and it will solve it. The Jewish Problem, the Gypsy Problem, the Homosexual Problem, the Handicapped Problem. It has the ethics of a slide rule.

To the ordinary mind—the highly conditioned, habituated, blindly reactive first few levels of consciousness—rationality is next to godliness. But as we delve deeper into consciousness, it is noted that "the tightly boundaried rational" is the hobgoblin of corner living, too small for the sacred whole.

Watch the process of thought. Don't get beached in the ordinary mind.

It is irrational to expect the ordinary mind to be rational enough to seek the mystery at the heart of the ordinary. It is just a problem-solving device almost exclusively involved with getting the candy from the table to your mouth. It is the way the mind gets what it wants as efficiently as possible with little or no ethical consideration. It is mindful only if punishment is involved. It makes a great servant, but a terrible master.

But before I totally besmirch the term "ordinary" as the commonly uninvestigated, let me say that it is in the moment-to-moment focus on the ordinary that the extraordinary is discovered. Going from the gross to the subtle, we discover ourselves underneath it all.

Indeed, because I misread the ordinary in the beginning, thinking I knew the difference, I saw too little and missed a rich opportunity. Acting as best man for a friend at his wedding at the San Francisco Zen Center in the 1960s, I met the dharma treasure Zen Master Suzuki Roshi and hardly connected with him. I was disappointed by his ordinariness. I couldn't recognize the invisibility of a perfectly balanced Tao, the miracle of the illuminated ordinary.

I learned a new level of respect for a much deeper level of the ordinary. Missing the mark with one whose writing and living example has been an inspiration to so many in the burgeoning spiritual movement in America repeatedly reminded me over time to clean the windows of my mindfulness.

The rational mind is as amoral as $2 + 2 = 4$, or -12 million. Efficiency is one of the highest virtues of the rational. But the rational suspects the non-self-centered quality of compassion. It is like those who came to complain to the Buddha about his teachings, or those who killed Socrates just to make sure, fearing that clarity might steal their children.

Sense the potential for cold indifference in our sometimes "mercilessly rational behavior." Listen instead to the heart. Be wholly irrational and in love. Drink from Kabir's cup. Dance with Rumi.

The healing never ends. Look yourself in the eye and say I forgive you—and mean it.

Perhaps the reason even the profoundly devoted "selfless" aspirants known in Buddhism as bodhisattvas do not recognize at times that they too are among those sentient beings they have vowed to liberate is because at this present stage of human evolution *we often don't feel particularly real to ourselves.*

To the ordinary mind others may somehow seem realer than ourselves, because when we say "I," we are referring to a flickering pattern of ideas, concepts, and fears, not to some solid, unchanging central figure within. No abiding permanent entity can be found within, only a wide stream of consciousness within which intermingling currents of thought attempt to create, define, and project who we think we should be, or who we think we are or might be, given the chance. We pretend to be real. We practice in the great rehearsal halls of the cortex before the mirror of our self-image.

But of course no amount of pretense can make us real. Only love makes things real.

The more we love, the more real we become.

We are so uncertain of ourselves, we cling to the rational. We have gone mad trying to be sane. We insist that "the furthest one need go is understanding." But understanding is not enough. It's just the beginning. Indeed, there is nothing we know that we could not know at a deeper level.

Ignoring what one teacher called "our buried treasure" would be a terrible price to pay just to appear more reasonable than you know the ordinary mind to be.

You have to be metarational to keep your reason, to open your ordinary mind to the experience of your extraordinary heart.

The ordinary mind spends its whole life in the skull; that is why identification with its contents is called small mind. Pretending that what is looking out is someone of value, it misses the precious truth of our true enormity.

Pretense is the common lie, performance our predominant strategy for survival. This desire to appear other than we know ourselves to be is very deep-rooted. Even now, every once in a while I get a glimpse of the mind as a starving two-year-old performing for a reward. We live this lie because it is the only truth we know. Our ordinary confusion mistakes knowledge for wisdom. It says we can know, but not be, God. But of course the truth is just the other way around. We can be God, but we are too big for small mind to find the words.

The will to live, to have, to be, maintains the common lie. It is addicted to becoming. And it insists that only something outside ourselves can bring happiness.

The will toward mystery reveals a deeper truth.

Interestingly enough, it is rumored that the wisdom for which Adam and Eve were expelled from Eden was the uncovering of the common lie. The truth imparted by the serpent expanded through the apple branches that there was no such thing as death. It said that the kingdom of heaven was within and that all we needed do was be compassionate and free within ourselves.

Although the myth has fig leaves and genitals in the telling, in truth Adam and Eve were ostracized for covering their heads before God. For realizing we are love, God, nothing more or less than Itself itself.

The ordinary mind would have us believe that ignorance is bliss, that Maya's Eden was paradise. Lulling us into the garden trap. The common lie says everything is just fine as long as I'm not the one in pain. The will toward mystery, like Suzuki Roshi, says, "Everything is perfect, but there is always room for improvement."

The ordinary mind creates reality to suit our misperceptions.

None of it really makes sense. The ordinary mind just pretends it does, so as not to incite a riot.

Sometimes we lie even when we mean to tell the truth. Sometimes we tell the truth and don't even know it, like a sightless person who, guessing the color of roses by their fragrance, answers, "The breath of God," and is never wrong.

We hope someday to tell the truth. But first we have to find out what it is.

And though we have lost our way ten thousand times, the longing just beyond the boundaries of the ordinary mind continues to trust and taste. We are irrationally hopeful, and that's often what it takes.

The way past the common lie lies straight ahead.

The ordinary mind, so full of becoming, has been on the make most of our lives.

On the make first for survival, then for supremacy. Driven by ambition, flatfooted, posturing to suit the fear, its guts growling with ego-hunger. Unable to be certain of the difference between pleasure and pain, it is constantly shapeshifting to fashion itself into the key that fits another's heart.

We have become rudderless and dissatisfied struggling so long for a place in line. On the make with friends and strangers, with praise and blame, with creation and destruction, with women, men, animals, and ghosts, with soil, plants, time, and space.

Even on the make in our prayers, and on our meditation pillow. On the make with God we bow our heads toward the sacred, seeking serotonin with each breath, our eyes aching with effort. On the make with Jesus and Buddha, with Death and Judgment Day.

Driven by becoming even in my dreams until one night I found myself sitting with a cooked dog across my lap. As I began picking at its cheek, surprised even in my dream that I should be doing such a thing, it was sweeter than I ever could have imagined!

Waking a bit dismayed, the heart whispered it was time to let go of the dog-eat-dog world. That it was time to sit down and just eat my own dog!

It was a letter of resignation!

To go beyond the ordinary mind is to go deeper than thought.

In Buddhism ignorance is often defined as the belief that you are the conditioned mind.

We have a mind, just as we have a body, but each is a manifestation of consciousness. What moves thoughts through the mind is precisely what moves the clouds across the sky. All are a part of the same continuum of creation unfolding. Mind and body float on the surface of the enormity of Being.

To go beyond the mind is to ever so irrationally and ever so reasonably go beyond our conditioning to the place, the logos, where unconditional love arises spontaneously.

You have to be more than rational to accept and dwell in the mystery. You have to love the truth in all its wild and subtle and indescribable forms.

We need to listen with the heart as we turn gently toward the mystery.

THE MIND SINKS INTO THE HEART

My mind keeps slipping out of the left side of my head. It leans away from the coldly self-protective and harmful rationality that insists, like most religions, that it is the only way.

Small mind becomes confused and claustrophobic when confronted with the enormity of its own Great Nature. It is forced to stop in its tracks and listen deeper to that which knows that God is not dead, but only broken-hearted Nietzsche's agonizingly rational attempt to love less, to feel less, to become a smaller target.

As the mind goes beyond the ordinary, beyond its conditioning and small knowing, it overflows its banks and becomes the heart. The boundaries of the rational dissolve into a feeling of great spaciousness that seems to be that state of being referred to in the New Testament as "the peace which surpasses understanding."

This vastness just beyond the understandings of our small selves is a joy that depends on nothing for its existence, a timeless clarity that has no history, no past or future, but only the living presence of Being, the suchness of "Itself itself."

Ironically, it is in the heart rather than the mind that we discover true rationality. That which seeks the best for all sentient beings. An inclination toward healing that even acknowledges the value of our pain. It learns to let go and trust the process. It knows there is an alternative to our well-guarded suffering.

It recognizes love.

The mystery is most audible in stillness.

The great Indian saint Ramana Maharshi, like Jesus, said, "Be still and know." Behind even "the still small voice within" there is yet a deeper quiet. A quiet that, once experienced, makes anything less than the whole seem almost a tragedy.

Even the most pleasant thought can be an unwelcome interruption in a peace that permeates the cells and settles a warring world. In the love that knows no other, anything other than love is just suffering. The restlessness and angst of being separate from our own Great Nature. Locked into a mind that thinks itself too small and trusts not the enormity swelling just beneath its crown.

TEN

retrieving the soul

This breaking through of what in Buddhist terms are called the hindrances, the qualities of mind that obscure the luminescence of our Great Nature, might in the devotional idiom be referred to as retrieving the soul.

There is an old saying: "You can save your ass or you can save your soul, but you can't save both." For a long time I felt I had forfeited my soul.

But the soul, like the heart, can never be lost, only obscured. The heart, like the sun, is always shining. We need do nothing to make it shine. Awareness is self-effulgent. All we need do is let go of what blocks it.

Another finger in the fist closed over our essence loosens and lets go. A letting go of "being loved" I would like to say, but it would be another of those lies we tell when we start talking too quickly about the truth. It perhaps lets go, instead, of what limited its ability to love. Each finger opening in this process of letting go increases our capacity to love. And brings the essence of Being to the surface.

There always seems to be a bit of discussion about what is the nature of the soul. There seems little consensus. What may be called soul in one belief system may be referred to in a very different manner in another way of thinking. To some it is the indwelling spirit. To others it is the karmic bundle, the repository of previous actions, attitudes, and intentions that produce this and future incarnations.

Some believe the soul to be eternal; others believe that time itself is impermanent. Eternity can have widely differing definitions depending on the peephole through which we are squinting.

For some, eternity means paradise with their beloved; for others, eternity is the time it takes and the births that must be taken to be wholly transformed into our indescribable original grace.

As one fellow put it, "One soul is big enough for all of us. In fact, that is the One to which so many belief systems separately refer."

Some say that a few moments after death we retrieve our soul. It sounded good, but I just couldn't wait. It is advisable in fact to begin as soon after birth as you remember.

The definition of soul that seems closest to most people's deepest experience is that of being "the witness," the awareness behind it all, the presence in presence.

Soul as watcher, the awareness that combines with what is near to produce consciousness.

To retrieve the soul is to regain consciousness.

That is why it is called awakening.

Awakening is not enlightenment, but it is a prerequisite. It is the breaking of the trance of blindly following conditioning. It is a coming into your own to find out who and what that might be.

We have literally passed out (or never passed in) and become unconscious. Now we must pass in (get fully born) to reestablish consciousness in the body/mind.

We need coax the light back with mercy and awareness.

First awareness must reenter the body—we must feel our feelings.

Then we must become aware we are aware.

And gradually we must at least consider forgiveness and kindness toward ourselves and perhaps another.

Eventually even love another, even love another as ourselves.

And ultimately we come to love for no reason whatsoever, to love wholly, unreasonably.

ELEVEN

getting born

When in the course of my soul-searching I first heard of and sought in meditation my "inner child," I sank through a level or two and found instead my shadow child, the hungry ghost.

Where I thought its heart would be there was a great emptiness. Not the spiritual emptiness I had hoped for, which dissolves all boundaries and removes all separation, but exactly its opposite. I found psychological emptiness, which finds all too readily the boundaries long ago constructed and constantly reinforced, within which resides a feeling of hopelessness and helplessness, and a pervasive vacuity. All that wished to remain unborn.

When I turned toward the mystery seeking to at last complete my birth, I found that child who wished he was never born still strapped all these years in that high chair, afraid to put his feet down on the ground.

Continuing the great treasure hunt for my life, I slowly introduced this more bewildered-than-angry ghost to the possibility of breaking the narrow confines of his imprisoned self-image.

This mindful investigation gradually became able to work with even quite painful emotions. As I focused on the feelings generated when I approached the child lost within, it became quite evident that every emotion, every state of mind, has its own distinctive body pattern.

Even when that child's residual fear or anger turned to terror or rage or when any "afflictive" emotion predominated, I could approach it with mercy and awareness without being distracted by its seductive thinking by focusing first on the concomitant sensations each state generated in the body's field of sensation.

When focused, I could follow my child's states of mind wandering through the body.

Observing in detail first its body pattern—this is a good example of relating *to* an object in consciousness instead of *from* it, breaking habitual identity with that state of mind—I was able to relate *to* this child instead of *as* this child, able to note his thoughts and feelings. And eventually recognized their incessant coming and going as a natural, actually impersonal process. In the stillness of meditation, I could see the energies of which these thoughts and feelings were composed, and meet them with mercy instead of fear and judgment.

When we receive emotion as sensation, the resistance that maintains the censor band between levels of consciousness falls away and the healing enters deeper.

In the course of this very gradual rebirthing, one day in meditation the shadow child came into view in the guise of an already world-weary, entirely untrustworthy twelve-year-old street hustler.

Although he preferred to be related to with fear and judgment so as to make himself all the more real, I tried to relate *to* him, rather than *from* him.

Acting as a completely autonomous personage, he turned toward me, the watcher, and actually tried to sell me a used car.

It was a perfect opportunity for healing, to relate with a merciful awareness instead of judgment and fear to that which felt so isolated and unloved. But I did not respond at first with love; instead, I reacted with embarrassment, shame, and fear.

There arose a desire to hide his birth, to lock it away in the turret or prison. To abort him or at least keep him from being born and embarrassing me in my well-crafted pretense.

Indeed, trying to sell me what was probably a stolen car was not the only time he addressed me directly in meditation. Once, when his image arose as I postured a shallow acceptance, he turned to me and said, "Even you don't love me!" And my gut turned to stone.

I could see in this closed reaction how speech and actions still arose from below the level of consciousness where I had stuffed them.

But the mystery usually provides an opportunity for compassion and completion if we pay attention.

When I turned to myself and tried to convince myself to buy a used car, I almost laughed out loud in that late-night meditation hall. My abdomen tightened to hold it back in the perfectly silent room in which perhaps forty people were doing a late-night sit.

As I watched myself congratulate myself for not disturbing the silence, a bench two sitters away began to creak as it slowly collapsed with a loud crack and groan. And then sank to the floor with a loud pop! The meditator thereon involuntarily exclaimed, "Oh, shit!" as his perch disappeared from under him. He spoke the sentiments of us all in great laughter at 2:00 A.M. watching hell or heaven with bright soul.

In the process of our awakening, it is fascinating to watch the falling away of the hindrances that is deep healing.

When I first came across this buried psychological momentum, I called it my shadow child. But as he was acknowledged and brought closer to the warming fire of clarity and kindness, that shadow child came more fully into the heart and was perceived with considerable empathy as a cornered child longing for the light.

It was that image of the unloved, partially born aspect of myself preparing to turn and face its untapped potential that signaled the possibility of actually forgiving and perhaps even loving myself.

The cornered child is profoundly attracted to the possibility of liberation.

When that cornered child begins to heal, learns to breathe and use love instead of pond water for its reflection, a very different relationship to the hindrances that hold him prisoner in painful identities becomes possible. The shadow pushes toward the light.

Purification is a process of letting go of whatever blocks the completion of our birth.

As I investigated the image and concept of the cornered child with a moment-to-moment awareness of the process of its unfolding, it became possible to follow its gestation to its origin in the broken-hearted outsider. The hungry ghost, its face pressed against the window, longing for birth and completion.

Investigating this ghost in my machine with a merciful awareness, I began to see the angry, even criminal street urchin for what it was— an archetypal tortured identity. A "leak-through from the shadow labyrinth," as I would later refer to it in the healing process of the dark night of the soul.

A well-established low personification whose seductive imagery has to be navigated in the course of wandering the lowlands of the underdream.

We tend to call the underdream the subconscious, but this is only because we are subattentive.

When one quiets in meditation, thoughts ordinarily too faint to perceive come into focus. Much of what is labeled as "subconscious" is there among the nearly translucent commentary. Beneath the gross is the subtle. Beneath any thought large enough to catch our attention are the subtle contributing factors that forced it to the surface: the tendencies from which it arose. With this subtle seeing we enter "the labyrinth of the unconscious," as early theorists might call it, at whose center an upwelling light, the psychospiritual equivalent of the birth canal, rises toward the mystery to complete its birth.

When Dante wandered his dark labyrinth, I suspect the hero was not really attempting to rescue his beloved, but himself. It was his soul, his clarity, he descended to retrieve. We cannot do it with anything we know, but only with how we love. Orpheus sang up the sun as his soul slipped away, so he went into the night to bring back the light.

As the healing unfolded, the parallel paths of the shadow world and the bright willing heart continued to intersect and even join at times, until the path with heart overcame the frightened. And the old (on a good day) lay as bedrock for the expanding new.

As the heart opened to this shadow child, this wandering ghost (it's why you can't get the mind to stop thinking), awareness invited him to complete his birth, to come whole into the world.

When the prodigal child returns to life, it begins at last to access the healing for which it originally took birth. And what results from that clarity and joy is that birth once again gains momentum as it begins gradually, even painstakingly, to cultivate acceptance of itself. Including those parts that serve us poorly. The mottled path through the hindrances to the heart.

When the cornered child is unshackled, he leaps joyously toward freedom. He becomes the child released within, the one that can't wait to get out and play. The one that has always been waiting like grace at your elbow. Born to listen to that still small voice, the freed child feels the bones melt in his chest when the heart, opened, bursts into flame.

Some refer to it as a second birth, or even rebirth, but I suspect it's just the completion of a process long ago abandoned.

And how few get born before they die!

And I came happily to refer to that once cornered child, with a term often used by Buddhists, as my karmic bundle.

While completing our birth we may experience what in Buddhism is called the "unborn quality of Original Mind," the mind before thinking, the boundless pasture in which anything at all might manifest.

This quality of unconditioned and unconditional openness is literally the beginning and end of it all. It is the boundless mind before it became conditioned, socialized, prejudiced, terrified. It is the spaciousness out of which love and compassion are born.

In the *Bhagavad Gita* it says the best of good fortune is to be born into the womb of a perfect yogi. But times have changed, and now we are called to give birth to ourselves.

I see all around me in the meditation hall cornered children getting born into Buddha realms. I see the healing child show through in each.

In one I see the child whose father died and no one spoke of it. He has learned to see and to love, but he still fears what he might say.

In another, tightly fisted, sits the bully child who feared sleep and became class president just to prove he could. He is learning to observe himself in a whole new way. He watches slowly as his palm comes into view. He thinks all he needs is the practice and he'll be all right. Leaving the meditation hall, he must suppress a slight compulsion to ring the teacher's big brass bell.

Across the hall in a corner sits the child so mistreated she believes too much in too little. But unbeknownst to her, there is a wisdom angel whispering which way to turn in the labyrinth. It brought her to this quiet place. Her child will soon be born.

There, unmoving on his psychic tiger skin, is the puritanical child who was taught to equate lust with the devil. He cannot comprehend how that old monk could have said he would prefer a hell with Jesus to a heaven without. He wears whites and means it, keeps the law, tells the truth, except about his recurring dream that Moses closed the sea, not opened it.

And on the other side of me is the sitting Buddha in whom remains the child locked out all night by his alcoholic parents. Having had to hide in the back streets of Houston until sunrise, he has got it down to two or three breaths a minute.

He, like the long-practicing Vietnam veteran sitting still as space next to him, has become as natural and effortless as the grass in spring. But they each still carry a picture of a dagger in their boot.

There is the triplet crowded in the womb and in the home, for whom there is no lap. She's made room for a thousand dying children in her arms. She really doesn't like to meditate much. Says half kidding she did it in another life, says she went through one as a madwomen too, knows her way around. Has softened the deathbed of millions.

And the child on the black *zafu* (meditation cushion) in priest's robes who is the only surviving sibling of a once large and busy household. He meditates like an orphan; it's good for his sittings. He no longer fears the fire in his belly. He accepts it all into the hospitality of his practice. And the children tell me he tells the best bedtime stories ever.

And the one who died at birth and seemed never to regain her appetite for life until her deep child came into being when it "heard the flute," what the God-drunken poet Kabir said was the entrance into the miraculous. The music was God and she was Lazarus up for a brand-new day! And ready for any ghosts that might come her way.

And on the *zafu* next to her the hungry ghost who's learning to feed others.

The Buddha said it does not matter how long you have forgotten, only how soon you remember.

When the hungry ghost is satiated, its heart is full and it begins to sing. It never was its stomach that was empty after all.

When ghost becomes spirit, we are fully born.

In the classic Hindu holy book the *Ramayana*, as Lakshman, Rama's brother, sat by the stream about to release his body into death, he looked back on his life and said, "It was like something I dreamed once, long ago, far away."

The heavens opened to receive him because there was nowhere else he wished to be.

What had broken open at the stoplight in Mexico City led away from the old. There was a process under way. With a vow that is operative to this day.

awakening a deeper life

TWELVE

the san francisco '60s

But before I get too far ahead of myself:

After some karmic catch-up, I arrived in San Francisco in the first week of 1965. The year was spent doing poetry readings and learning from the extraordinary North Beach poetry scene. I finalized the chapters and integrated illustrations from various alchemical texts for the publication of *Synapse: Visions of the Retinal Circus*. It was a year of new community and an expanded sense of together action.

The cornered child had turned his face to the light.

Helping to edit a small magazine, I was invited in 1966 to join the editorial staff of the newly formed psychedelic *San Francisco Oracle*. I found a natural fit in the Haight-Ashbury fellowship of seekers, visionaries, and a few intergalactic emissaries. This was the family I had left home to find.

It was a remarkable time. Across the country ages, classes, races, and sexes momentarily bonded in a common cause to end the war in and around us and search for peace. We too in the Elysian fields across the bay could see that the only way to stop the war was to be like Arjuna in the *Gita*, who stood between warring factions, with loved ones on both sides, and suggested we consider first ending the battle within ourselves. Reminding us that our real enemy was not ourselves or each other, but the deadly emanations of the common lie that insists we are not essentially peace.

In 1967 in "Notes from the Genetic Journal" in the *Oracle* I wrote: "Suspended between supernova and atomic dervish, I am Man, center of the Universe, disproving Copernicus after all, cosmic acrobat trapezing on the tendency toward rebirth. Poised between whirring mass at either end of infinity." I think that pretty much describes my condition at the time.

Working with so many visionary artists and writers propelled my sense of a world community actually capable of peace and service. It was a community whose highest value was self-knowledge and concern for the weakest and most disenfranchised among us.

The *Oracle* staff of poets and visionaries met and exchanged ideas with some of the prime movers of the time: Allen Ginsberg, Alan Watts, Ken Kesey, Michael McClure, Gary Snyder, Lew Welch, Lenore Kandel, Gavin Arthur, Richard Grossinger, Sun Bear, Richard Brautigan, Lawrence Ferlinghetti, Ali Akbar Khan, and Timothy Leary, who reminded everyone to tune in, turn on, and drop out just around the time that service work was dropping me back in.

Service accompanied my awakening.

I started to print and distribute free meditation books under the name Unity Press with the help of friends, from Ron Polte to Bill Graham, and the support of many of the San Francisco bands, from the Kingston Trio to the Grateful Dead, who provided funds for paper and binding. Later we published the poetry of a death-row inmate in the Nevada state prison for whom I acted as liaison with the media and legislature to bring national attention to his fasting-unto-death protest about the death penalty. After a few weeks they force-fed him and sent me a letter saying my visiting and contact privileges on death row had been revoked because I was a "bad influence."

One of the phenomena of the times was what was called the acid test. It was a surreal carnival of chemically supported consciousness play. Usually the sound track was provided live by the Grateful Dead. The refreshment was a Kool-Aid concoction in a shiny new plastic trash barrel. The Merry Pranksters' world-class psychedelic tour bus *Further* was tethered just out back. Neal Cassady, its sometimes pilot, in a tight dervish not far away. It was the delight of community and the company of fellow travelers at a time when "fellow traveler" had come to mean something quite different than it had a few years earlier at the McCarthy hearings.

Called down to L.A. for the Watts Acid Test, I stayed with the circus at Wavy Gravy's house. That evening in the strobe-lit, music-blasted, energy-popping, tie-dyed converted warehouse, as the carnivalers floated on the dance floor, standing next to a friend who was breaking ampules of pure LSD into the orange Kool-Aid, I was handed a broom handle and it was suggested I stir the cosmic brew. As I stirred the second batch, the concentrated liquid being poured in splashed on the back of my hands. The big top was about to go up.

The Grateful Dead was recording each of six sets and playing each under the next (or so it seemed to me at the time). By the end of the evening, on the sixth set, with the five previously recorded sets played simultaneously back behind them, I took my overloaded senses out to the bus and cooled out with Neal for a while. One of the remarkable things about Neal was you could never tell whether he was "dosed" or not. He was "twice normal," with a realness about him that had long appealed to the right brain of many. Just as after a poetry reading, feeling a bit dissatisfied and wondering if perhaps I should be reading more dramatically, he said to me, "Just read it the way you wrote it." Speaking the simple truth with an almost Zen directness, he was often inspiring.

In the midst of throwing rusted iron scraps discovered sticking out of a barren field into the back of my Jeep pickup truck one afternoon "because it's a shame to waste it," he stopped abruptly. "Oh, shit. We've got a book party to go to at my old wife's house."

We were in a bit of a haze, so I never did find out which author his ex-wife was opening her home to. But as well as I can recall after joining the considerable circle of his acquaintanceship, leaning with us against the purple dragon were a few San Francisco poets and company, media and New York publishing folk, self-lubricating cognoscenti, and a few gallery types. And a row of Harleys and leather jackets. It was like something between a Leonard Bernstein Park Avenue soirée and a meeting of the local chapter of the Hell's Angels. A very congenial atmosphere, "as long as none of the poets turn violent," a biker cracked.

Giving Neal's girlfriend and her friend a ride from San Francisco down the coast route to meet him at Kesey's La Honda digs, where a considerable gathering was occurring, I felt the car begin to swerve. The steering on the Volkswagen bug did not respond on a curve. The car rode the guardrail for about seventy-five feet and, becoming momentarily airborne, flipped over, rolling down the steep embankment and stopping upside down on a ledge halfway to the Pacific below. Luckily I was thrown clear before the roof caved into the steering wheel. Amazingly, the women were barely scratched.

It was only later when the highway patrol reported, after inspecting the wreckage, that there was nothing amiss with the steering apparatus that the women told me they thought it might have been their fault. When I said that was not possible, they confessed that they had half-heartedly committed to taking part in some sort of black mass with a long-dismissed local satanist who, when they withdrew, had said in anger, "If you drive, you will fly!"

Who knows what all that was about. Another "big don't know" from the mystery. But it seems less surprising within the context of the times.

I was told later that back at Kesey's place—which we never reached—a true sign of those times was manifest: so many had used the bathroom facilities, they had backed up. Allen Ginsberg, needing to use the toilet, was stymied by the bowl nearly overflowing with fecal matter. Standing before and needing badly to use the unusable toilet, he began to chant. Passing by, Neal leaned in and said, "Geez, Allen, don't you believe in anything?!"

Neal and I spoke often of Mexico and his strong desire to "get down there as quick as possible." He lit up with tropical fantasies and encouraged me to come along. But concerned that my illegal antics from three years before might catch up with me there, I said I'd wait to hear his tales of wonder when he returned. A month later with a brave band of Merry Pranksters he headed south of the border. And a month later he died.

At the very periodic *Oracle*, meetings with remarkable men and women defined the possibility of a world at peace with itself. Richard Alpert, just before he became Ram Dass, and a lifelong friend, Rolling Thunder, the Shoshone medicine man whose prophetic aside to me about my future came to pass; Chinmayananda, from whom the bright Hindu heart was transmitted; and the precious time with Buckminster Fuller, his four- or five-hour rambling-genius talks igniting a free-flowing rapport between hemispheres of the brain.

And that dear heart, early interpreter of Zen, Alan Watts, on whose houseboat I was staying while working with Armando Busick on the illustrations for a new book on the night Alan died a few miles away at a friend's farm.

An odd scene comes to mind of coming to visit Alan one Saturday afternoon and his introducing me to a fellow he said was a "big man on campus in Philadelphia." And his taking me aside and saying, "Get this guy out of here. He feels all wrong!"

When I took him out for lunch, he reminded me of some from an earlier, less trustworthy lineage. His name was Ira Einhorn. He was later accused of murder. It was not surprising that Alan picked up on this fellow's dark underpinnings. What was surprising, or more accurately disheartening, was that Einhorn's considerable number of followers didn't, and so much hunger for true wisdom and life expansion had gone as misdirected in the City of Brotherly Love as it had in Saigon.

THIRTEEN

service as shared healing

When I lived in jazz Miami, I occasionally went to a jai alai game in the sports arena.

Leaving one evening before the last match was over, I stopped at the large glass doors leading out into the parking lot seeing there was a monsoon downpour. As I waited for a break in the clouds, I noticed about a hundred feet away, standing in the pouring rain, a blind young man trying to retrieve his obviously frightened and wary seeing-eye dog. It may have been a rather new relationship, as they clearly were not yet coordinated in their actions. Each time the dog would reapproach, the boy would step forward onto the dog's left front paw. The dog would then retreat with a howl, which only made the young man cry and plead harder.

I wanted to run out into the rain and help them, but I hesitated because it seemed they were slowly working it out and my approach might have reexcited the confusion.

I watched with relief as the young man, getting off his feet, kneeled on the wet pavement as the dog ran into his arms. They held on to each other like long-lost lovers.

As the crowd began to leave the arena, attendants came out to the young man with towels and warmth.

From such moments of empathy, the heart's imperative to relieve suffering became unmistakable. Nurtured by an increasing sense of being part of the greater community, the expanded family of the heart, I felt drawn to service.

For a long time I took more than I gave.

Where once I thought if I was not number one I was nothing, I came to see the world with kinder eyes. Where once I had looked at people for what I could get from them, now I looked at them for what they might need.

The opening of the heart, a karma yoga, is the reversal of that grasping. Karma yoga is the art of returning everything to its source, of holding nothing separate from the heart, of acting in a way that is beneficial to all involved.

The wounded energy that had once acted out so hurtfully, the momentum (as good a word for karma as any I can imagine) that had once served so few, now turned with relief and confidence toward the path (the karma yoga) of compassionate service.

The two aspects of my path that led me forward were practiced on the ground of service.

If at first I meditated to be a good meditator, that eventually evolved into just wishing to be a whole human being.

To become a whole human being, we must first get right with the earth and the animal spirits thereon.

Then we can serve those in pain in hospitals, prisons, and healing centers. We can be present for the grieving and share growth.

Perhaps it is when we give as much as we take that we truly become human beings, instead of ghosts.

Ondrea, my wife and spiritual partner, refers to "the gift in the wound"—one aspect of which leads people in the course of their healing to recognize all the others suffering about them. By converting the fear of *my* pain to compassion for *the* pain, by moving from the personal to the universal, an experience that can diminish one expands to a sense of participation in the greater family.

To share the healing, we take another merciful step into the pain and compassion of the world.

During the early years of practice-as-purification, still detoxifying from hungry-ghost activity, I would sometimes wake with intense heat radiating from my body. Not night sweats, though those too may be a minor key in the alchemy of detoxing the heavy to the light.

The heat broke my fever.

During these "heatings" I was often not able to return to sleep for an hour or more before I cooled.

In this alchemy, as in many chemical reactions, heat is a catalyst, for in true alchemy it is the alchemist who is transformed. Once awakened, he or she distills the solid world into its luminous essence.

It is the recognition of the healing power of service.

In the healing process, service unites what is within with what is outside.

When first we identify with our role as giver, even this positive identity can make us smaller. There is only a meeting of minds. Very two-dimensional! Very dualistic: giver and receiver, I and other, success and failure. Not much room for anything else.

But as the intention to be of service ripens over time, the interaction may become heart to heart. Healer and healed meeting in the intuitive spaciousness of the shared heart. Each awareness gravitating toward the other, creating an even larger consciousness.

Service to the dying is no different than any other relationship. Just two people together. But there's more to it than pillow thumping when we act as what is called *kalayana mita*, a spiritual friend.

The beginning of the path of service is commitment to the practice of noninjury, such as is reflected in the Hippocratic oath: while serving, do no harm.

And a remembering that as the Kyoto Zen Master said, "Reminding others of the enormity of their own Great Nature is the highest service one can offer another."

Before the osmosis of the heart, before energy can flow unimpeded by self-congratulation or possession, we need to learn to share, as it is said, "in a royal manner." To practice generosity by at times giving of the best we have until the giving disappears into thankfulness along with the sense of ownership or even pride.

As the chasm of I and other, across which service flowed, slowly narrowed, I was no longer busy being good, pridefully serving the needy. Service was no longer at the top of my resume. I was less "glad to help" and more simply offering energy where it seemed called for.

First we serve, then we become service. It is a lot like prayer: first you pray, but eventually your life becomes the prayer. First you sing, then you become the song. Gandhi said, "My life is my message."

FOURTEEN

sanctuary

When I first met spiritual teachers, there was a deep intoning. Something in me wanted to touch my forehead to their feet. I knew we had work together.

But before I could do that, I had to connect with the earth, to "bring the earth to witness," as they said of the Buddha's touching the ground to dispel the distractions that were assailing him. There are many initiations along the way to becoming a whole human being, but first and last is our connection with the earth and animal spirits.

Seeking to share the ground of all sentient beings after the years at the *Oracle* and the Haight-Ashbury celebration, I took service to the earth.

Finding my place in the food chain, I tended the Canelo Hills Wildlife Sanctuary in southern Arizona for the Nature Conservancy. I had a horse, a badge, and a typewriter.

In the journals that later became *Planet Steward* I wrote:

In green meadow picking the apples, pears and quince offered by the frontier homesteader buried eighty years beneath the porch. The bark-

ing of the Samoyed attracted me through the shoulder-high Johnson grass, bordering walnut trees and across the stream. Up the side of an outcropping of lichened rock into the forest of twisted live oak I saw the dog sitting, barking, tail wagging, having treed a coatimundi. Her two-foot tail swishing at first made me think the dog had cornered a puma, until her long snout swung my way. The harsh chattering of denial and warning shook the limb she has backed out on. Her cat-round eyes stared into mine in plea and survival threat, though she could easily have destroyed this dog who so gleefully awaited my praise. . . . Instead, the hard edge of my voice lowered dog's ears against furry head, and he crouched confused, scolded in the warm green shade of victory in which he stood, conqueror pulled away. The coatimundi, large tropical relative of raccoon, bounded to higher ground, into the safety of grandfather oak. Prattling in the midst of sanctuary.

Returning to the house, I checked the reference books for more details on this golden creature, the first one I had met. I went into the Bird Room to feed the second bird I had taken in during the two months I had been tending and tended by this wildlife sanctuary. The first was a mockingbird found beneath thunder apple tree in the midst of a hard summer rain who had long since mended and been freed though it still was about. Flying down from the cottonwoods for a shirtpocket raisin. Fed a dozen times a day, another member of the planet family.

The latest charge was a wounded Cassin's Kingbird brought by a neighbor two days before. Shot with a BB gun by his eleven-year-old brother. Its wing bones were broken, the flesh torn beneath left wing. Just that morning after eating, beginning to settle in a bit, nearly taking the raisin offered. Now dead—still warm, passed from his body less than an hour before. Taking him back outside into flightless space to bury him.

Walking toward the stream, his back nestled against my palm, his yellow breast turned toward the empty sky. He reminded me of the golden flesh of ten thousand children burning in the jungles of Viet Nam. Reminding me that what killed this bird kills man. That the trigger-finger mind seeking to prove itself in the death of another is the suicide of consciousness. The dissociation of man kind & unkind from nature, removed from the life force percolating through. What killed this slowly stiffening bird kills the planet, kills itself, conquers man, locks him in the least realms of mind, anchored to his fears. Blocked from the light of the living continuum in which he might find his joy.

The bird laid to rest in the limbcrotch of an old cottonwood beside the stream, covered with the dead bark of ancient willows . . . all white buffaloes absent . . . left to return to that from which he sprang.

Namo Amida Butsu.

Sometimes the full moon reminds me of cows.

Waking in sanctuary one morning on the high plateau grasslands, across a cold October sky, came the rising lament of bereft mothers, like Whitman's late by the lilacs heard.

It was the day they ship the calves.

From a nearby ranch yipping cowboys and the fearful bellow of cattle. Bright red tandem trailer pulled up to the loading chutes.

Calves separated from mother cows, hauled to feed-lot pens, stuffed fat as Strasbourg geese. "Four or five pounds a day." 800 pounds by kill time 5 months away. "Highest price per pound yet! 2 cents more for steers, a penny for heifers. Steers tenderer, heifers fatten quicker . . . "

Myacined and drugged so the fever never comes until slow-eyed death creeps like a French executioner at dawn to drag them bawling to the adrenaline mists of the slaughterhouse. The groaning butchery to be done. The muscled hammer or the sly pistol right between the eyes. And down they go, meat permeated with dread and trembling passed on across the dinner table to the grumbling, overcrowded, overstuffed denizens of the supermarket. The well-bibbed knife and

*fork attempting to dignify the kill. The omnivore eating the herbivore
with table manners. Fear of the dark in a roasting pan.*

*On the way to the morning mailbox heavy necks of young steers
swing my way. Pink-rimmed eyes peering between the slats. Glassy
brown eyes into mine. Then swing back again, resigned.*

*And the first prayer is recited over their meat as I begin counting
heads, then stop, knowing their lives were bred for dying. Their conception guided toward the "calf crop."*

*These broad-faced Herefords chewed unconsciously by broad-
faced broken-hearted America. Swallowed into the dark interior, taking on the animal consciousness digested. The ritual cannibalism of
the Eucharist, eating Christ's flesh to absorb his knowing, fallen a few
octaves to pink-eyed Burger World and the herd mind of city.*

*The thought rising that when we received our sustenance from the
silently hunted forest, the city-pueblo was a planet-hearted community, more of the nature of the sweet wild beasts that supported and
religioned life.*

*The hunter becomes what he hunts, the butcher the butchered,
the predator the prey. Each mouthful takes us one step farther from
the sun.*

*Into evening the mother cows bawling, bulging, rebred, full of
fresh meat once again.*

*Bawling for the calves departed in red truck early in the afternoon.
Aching cows' teats full of milk for sucklings lost to supermarket cello-
phane, "best side up."*

*All night an urgency, a cry to the half moon. All night cows calling
out. One more persistent than the others, inconsolable.*

*Between the rancher's house and the empty loading chutes some-
times just one, then three or four, unlike the calling of birds or wolves
an animal cry not for territory or mating, but the solemn bellow of
despair like the intermittent sobbing at a wake.*

*Sitting through the night before a juniper fire in the room with the
saguaro ceiling. Immersed in a chorus of lamentation. Reflecting that*

it's not a matter of meat or meat eating, it's just our drowsy blindness
and the unnecessary suffering of our fellow beasts.

On the first designated Earth Day, in 1970, living with considerable pleasure on the sanctuary, I was invited to give presentations at Cornell and Syracuse University.

Going from the verdant luxury of peace-on-earth to the cacophonous anxiety of the university was a bit unnerving.

But it was heartening to see that some students seemed to realize that perhaps Earth Day meant love your neighbor as yourself. That perhaps everything does.

It was a delight to see how many were beginning to serve others, how many were becoming part of the whole.

Each year I am reminded that another Earth Day approaches. Downwind from the end of the world, each bird song reminds me. Each fox and squirrel, each raven, each grandchild laughing or crying reminds me of my earthen body. And the spirit that depends on nothing, that can be obscured, but not polluted. The spirit in the tortoise too, on whose carapace our spirit ancestors visualized the earth transported through the seasons of the mystery.

FIFTEEN

the precious teachings

In Tibetan Buddhism they speak of the dharma, the teachings, as "the priceless gem, the pearl beyond value." Indeed, perhaps the greatest gift one might be born with is a longing for deeper truth, an appreciation of the wisdom teachings. And the will to carry them out.

We recently heard a story from a therapist about a fellow who had been in Auschwitz and after the war was having a very difficult time in his healing process. With all the issues and hard memories he had to deal with, one in particular seemed to personify for him his extended torture and imprisonment. As much animosity as he felt toward the guards, he held his greatest hatred for another inmate. One who had somehow sneaked into the concentration camp a small Hebrew prayer book, which very many wished to use or at least hold. But he would only let them see or touch it if they paid him with a bit of food or a piece of clothing. Perhaps their only pair of shoes. Many hastened their death because they bartered away their last possessions for a glimpse at the sacred words. The images of their frozen, ruined bodies haunted the patient, and his hatred for "this traitor to God" knew no bounds.

Until one day, years into his healing process, a remarkable insight arose. He realized, as his heart burst open, that the object lesson to be received was not how horrifically one human can treat another, but what the borrowers of the book had known all along: that words of the spirit, that contact with the mystery, is worth more than life itself.

And as he integrated this enormous insight, he came to realize that the heart is even more precious than the body.

My rabbi didn't have a hair on his body. A high fever as a child, I was told.

He had a uniquely soft look about him. He was one of my first truly gentle adults.

When I would question some of the tenets of the faith—his son and I were schoolmates, so I had at times a bit more access to him—he always said, "It's not as important to be a good Jew as it is to be a good human being."

Even that "the truth" was open to discussion was mind-altering, because at last the subjects of the heart had been broached.

God and Aristotle, Moses and manna were up for grabs, as, beyond words, he demonstrated that mercy comes not from some distant divine power broker, but from the very human heart. His presence and bearing served as living options. They were world-opening teachings.

I met Rudi, my first spiritual teacher, as, strolling down Seventh Avenue, I gazed at a twenty-foot-long reclining bronze Buddha in the window of his Asian art shop. When I entered, a very round, red-faced angelic turned toward me and said, "You know Jesus wasn't only white!" And he took me by the hand without the least introduction and guided me to a glass case from which he withdrew what appeared to be a rather old scroll. He unwound it to reveal to me an ascetic Asian Jesus draped on the cross.

He could not have chosen a more engaging opening. I trusted him instantly; he appeared to me as true spirituality rather than false religion.

Our relationship continued for some years and often included sitting together on folding chairs across the sidewalk from his Oriental art shop, observing the people who passed between us and the reclining Buddha. He spoke of "seeing people as states of mind" and gradually taught me to read their states as they passed by.

One of his first and most needed teachings repeated to me dozens of times was "Assume nothing!" (Which was my first opening into the teachings that would later be refined for me by Zen Master Sueng Sahn in the endless opening and depth of the "Don't Know" teachings.)

On the one hand, Rudi was teaching me to be more intuitive, cultivating heart-to-heart communication, while, on the other, exhorting that I take none of this as completely real. "Question everything and listen with the inner ear." Insisting that I know nothing for long and trust only those understandings that convey the mind into the heart.

Rudi's rather large head kept changing shape. He would ask me to check it out every once in a while just to be sure he was not just imagining it. His tectonic plates were definitely shifting. He would have been a phrenologist's dream.

My time with him expanded the universe and gradually changed my definition of gravity.

Gravity continued to expand as I sat most mornings during the Haight-Ashbury days contrasting three different translations of the *Bhagavad Gita* (the "Glorious Song"), seeking the living truth by comparing the uneven breathing of various translators. The long Hindu-influenced morning quiet time expanding into a Buddhist meditation practice, a commitment to the healing miracles of mindfulness.

How well architected the mystery that, though it was Buddhism that first posited awakening and stimulated my imagination in the mid-'50s, it was ten years later, sitting on my bedroom floor with the *Bhagavad Gita* in my lap, that my body began to teach me further to meditate.

With the mind strongly drawn into the heart while reading the great holy book, upon closing my eyes the breath seemed to begin breathing itself in and out of my heart. I took that as the closest thing to meditation instructions I was going to get at the time.

Reading the *Glorious Song* quieted the hungry ghost and opened my hungry heart. It made the world sacred. Safe for the further exploration of the breath passing in and out of the center of my chest.

I continued with the heart-breath practice on and off for a few years, until in 1967 a poet friend with whom I had shared needles and a case of hepatitis years before in New York City, having become a Buddhist monk on returning from Burma, brought me a copy of the *Satipattana Sutra* and the mindfulness teachings of Mahasi Sayadaw. From which a lifetime of mindfulness meditation practice ensued.

He said it was the best teaching he received in the monastery. And the best he had to share. And it was. It was a treatise that so drew me toward my spacious center, the luminous field of awareness, that we later published it as the first of our Unity Press free books.

I met my first Buddhist meditation teacher, Sujata, after I had been meditating for five years without benefit of an instructor. My guide had been the tattered Xerox of the Mahasi Sayadaw's *vipassana* (mindfulness or insight meditation) instructions.

Though *vipassana*, mindfulness practice, was not originally intended for psychological healing but rather the development of a nonjudgmental, clear-sighted, "choiceless" awareness, it is one of the most powerful tools for psychological clarification available. In the course of penetrating the hindrances to clear seeing, the obstacles to the heart, mindfulness defines them and makes them susceptible to healing.

Meeting mind moment after mind moment with a merciful aware-ness gradually brings the object of mindfulness into balance. Mindful-ness harmonizes each part of us with the whole. In the arising of silent understanding there is transmitted one of the great insights of spiritual, and particularly mindfulness, practice: *awareness heals.*

AWAKENING

To awaken is to become aware.

To become aware is to put that awareness to work on the further awakenings that lead toward liberation.

We are born with a mind that needs watching.

The mind cannot be left unattended. It constantly wanders off, attracted by nearly any shiny object. Entranced by light and movement. More than once I have had to drag it away from the neon tattoo parlor.

The mind changes all by itself.

One moment mind wants one thing, the next moment the oppo-site. It thinks one thing and says something quite different. It alter-nately likes and dislikes the same person, place, or thing. It is capable of even loving and hating the same object. It is often conflicted. One moment the mind suggests an ice-cream sundae, then fifteen minutes later turns to you and says, "I wouldn't have done that if I were you!"

It is infinitely insecure and constantly uncertain. It rearranges per-ception to fit the substituted dream.

The mind has a mind of its own.

It wishes to appear other than it imagines itself to be. It tests the brainpan for an echo from some true God or solid self, but when none is recognized, the loneliness creates an image of someone listening. We are that idea of ourselves.

Addicted to pretense and the common lie, it has made strategic moves away from who it really is. And then it forgets.

Any idea of who we are is too small for the whole of us.

We are evolution-incomplete completing itself. Bragging and cow-ering, judging and pretending, the superficial conditioned common mind nonetheless struggles to go beyond itself. The will toward mys-tery has an urge to unite, to love and be loved, to enter into the mys-tery of self and other. To go past such duality to the One that lies beyond thought or thinker, to the heart of the unspeakable wholeness and delight that patiently awaits our inward arrival.

We suffer from a case of mistaken identity.

We mistake ourselves for "mind only," the content of our mind.

We try to be "someone" because we fear we are no one.

The mind in conflict drags that aspect of itself it cannot love to a therapist. The therapist helps it see the repeated patterns of its content and what part it imagines itself to be and what it rejects. On a good day it can connect the heart with the disheartened.

When we explore this condition a bit deeper with a spiritual friend, the process to these patterns may become evident. And we see we only think we are the content when we relate *from* (identify with) that thought. But when we relate *to* it, we see that thought is just a flash in the brainpan. A single frame in the mind movie, a moment of content in a process of thought. We watch thoughts think themselves, unfolding from moment to moment all by them-selves.

If you think you are the mind, stop it RIGHT NOW . . . Or does it continue its commentary on its own?

To be able to observe the theater, not just continue "being on stage," to become the space in which our drama unfolds, not mistaking ourselves for the dialogue or the stage directions, we need enter the underlying energy that animates it all.

There are many levels of meaning to terms like "the spirit of the moment"; we mean each of them.

When we know the difference between thought and thinking, the mystery begins to solve itself. Thought is the opening imagery of the movie; what follows, the whole unfolding of the comic drama, is thinking.

Original sin is attachment to our ordinary suffering.

We nail ourselves to the cross because we have forgotten. The nails are produced from within. They grow outward from the palm. Our unwillingness to forgive ourselves serves perfectly as stigmata. We say it must be this way, because somehow we have come to believe that crucifixion is easier than love.

SIXTEEN

sujata

Having been graced with thirteen months at the sanctuary and the birth of my second child, I was hoping to serve humans.

In 1971, I left the sanctuary and returned to Santa Cruz, California, where we soon transformed Unity Press, the free press that had distributed without charge meditation and socially conscious books in the San Francisco '60s, into a conventional publishing company.

Over the next five years we published, among other artful and healing texts for human and animal, several contemporary meditation teachings.

After I had worked a few years with injured birds—learning from the wildlife-rescue programs that cleaned oiled seabirds and treated birds such as hawks and owls broken-winged from flying into power lines—even aiding in the publication of Mae Hickman's long-caring work *Care of the Wild Feathered and Furred*.

In the early '70s, Sujata, a young Buddhist monk whose book I was editing, became a very strong influence on me to "take the practice deeper." His guidance was crucial to my evolution.

Committed to a daily mindfulness practice and eventually longer meditation retreats, I got greater traction on the path.

My first intensive was a five-day silent meditation retreat, sitting and walking eighteen hours a day, with an interview with the teacher for thirty minutes each afternoon.

After the retreat and my first glimpse of emptiness, the egoless vastness at the center, as I was taking out my car keys I asked from a delighted bewilderment, "I'm going to get behind the wheel, but who's going to drive home?"

Sometimes grace may not always be pleasant, but it always brings us closer to our true nature.

And completing your birth can be messy work.

In the first year of "heavy practice" with Sujata my back broke out in large boils. Without much understanding at the time of the deeper processes of purification and harmonization possible from the practice, I nonetheless felt at first an excited sense of accomplishment, no matter how purulent. I couldn't tell if this sort of pride was a reaction to, or a cause of, these protuberances.

During this process I was reminded that the Greek author Nikos Kazantzakis, while working tirelessly on the manuscript for *The Last Temptation of Christ*, experienced large boils on his body. When he went to his advisor to find the cause of these signs of toxification (or perhaps detoxification), he was told of the experiences of the desert fathers. Those contemplative monks bent on purification of the soul, or what might be called absolute clarity of vision, also developed hot, engorged blemishes during the course of their intense practice.

Perhaps the hindrances received by mercy rather than fear permitted them to rise physically to the surface as well. The body draining off the toxicity of so many betrayals and self-cruelties.

No one can truthfully say practice is easy, only that it can free us from so much other uneasiness.

Buddha said it is easier to overwhelm a thousand foes on the battle-field than overcome the hindrances.

WHEN EVENING IS NIGH

In the course of spiritual practice it is not uncommon for one's intense purification to include finding oneself in a long dark hopeful night before the possibility of an infinite dawn.

There are a few dark nights one passes through in the course of spiritual practice. When awakening to the experience of Oneness we also partake of the grief of the world that is the breaking through of compassion and wisdom.

As my practice gained momentum over the next few years of study with Sujata, in 1973 I got more than I bargained for, and just what I needed.

Sitting in my cottage next to Santa Cruz Point, within hearing of the Pacific, on my meditation bench in the corner of my bedroom, I could feel "the awe-full truth that liberates" approaching.

Years of learning to let go of the impediments to deeper seeing had allowed boundaries and censor bands to be crossed. Awareness sank farther and farther into unexplored territory, uncovering the suppressed and repressed material of a lifetime, and perhaps lifetimes.

Though much psychological clarification had been accomplished over the years, as additional levels were exposed in meditation, yet a more miraculous and more painful healing was awaiting.

As a lifetime of resistance and posturing melted, I fell through into the repressed, but no longer suppressed, darkness.

Entering into what seemed a thousand lifetimes of loss and disappointment, I found myself in the realm of primitive fear and ancient unresolved grief.

Dissolving into the reservoir of grief, the great salty sea the Buddha said was the accumulation of all the tears we have shed for all the losses in all our lives.

And I drowned through realms of grief from the personal to the universal, in just the way most growth occurs.

And the heart remembered from kachinas and Medicine Buddhas the teaching from so many traditions that refers to the need for us to realign the heart center in times of grief. The need to attend to the very sensitive point at the center of the chest, called the grief point in one tradition, the wounded heart chakra in another, and conception 17 in a third.

What became a very powerful therapeutic, spirit-revealing grief meditation developed over time, as I pressed firmly with the thumb into the very tender spot in the middle of my sternum. The grief point, after releasing a considerable amount of energy, converts at the touch point of the heart. As our universal heart slowly absorbs our personal pain, there is a great sigh of letting go.

But before *my* pain might dissolve into *the* pain, I had an ocean of sorrow to cross.

In Buddhism the word for suffering is *dukka*. Grief is *dukka*, disappointment is *dukka*, loss is *dukka*. *Dukka* is acknowledged as the result of attachment, the holding and/or resistance to the contents of the moment. When what we want does not come, or when what we love departs, we experience *dukka*. But when the student asks, "If *dukka* is personal pain, what then do you call that universal dissatisfaction arising from inborn desire some call 'existential angst,' the intrinsic grief at a sense of incompleteness?" Teacher smiles the smile that acknowledges this terrible/wonderful world and simply says, *"Dukka, dukka!"*

What was arising was not just my grief, but *the* common grief as well. Not just the personal, but the universal sorrow. The infinite insecurity of a centerless mind. An anguish so great it stretched from a lifetime's accumulated losses all the way to the terror of not being.

Anything held to leaving rope burns as it was pulled beyond my grasp by incessant change.

Through the night, primal fear and helplessness. Impotent rage and distrust. Shame, doubt, and hopelessness: the same chorus line of grief and longing that presented itself beneath Buddha's shade tree. But Buddha reached down and "called the earth to witness" the purity of his intention.

Brailling through the harsh shadow play it became evident that all guilt, all anger, all fear, doubt, and distrust are manifestations of unresolved grief, both personal and universal. The latter the price of getting born, the former the cost of not completing that process.

Over the next days I was at times hopeless and seemingly helpless experiencing again and again a world of suffering within and around me. Experiencing even the origins of those earlier suicidal rumblings at the bottom of the underdream.

The old was falling away, but the new had not yet presented itself. I was lost between realms in what sometimes seemed the dark night of the soul.

At times I felt I had bitten off more than I could chew, that a certain spiritual bravado on my part had led me astray. In those moments I would have readily traded this startling new clarity for my old ignorance and denial.

I became lost in the underdream playing itself out just below the well-edited contents of the ordinary mind. The ghost wandering the bottom of the id, roaming the corridors of the shadow labyrinth, the dark, often unpleasant, sometimes violent, survival-oriented, now Cro-Magnon imagery repeated in the passing shadows. The result of having taken birth in our present, evolutionarily incomplete human form. A realm of consciousness, like war or peace, always present, but seldom acknowledged that, deep in shadow, sends coded messages as impulses to the surface.

I wandered a realm that, when one becomes stuck in identification with its ironically impersonal though threatening imagery, becomes for Christians purgatory or hell; and for Buddhists perhaps the realm of the wrathful deities. Or what the Buddha might have called simply "mind only."

What I imagined was going to take a few days of investigation continued on this horizonless plain for months.

After nearly a month of psychological spelunking through daily intervals of angst and confusion, trusting Thomas Merton's assurance that "true prayer is learned when prayer has become impossible and the heart has turned to stone," I asked a friend if I might borrow his unused cabin in the redwoods for a short retreat.

When I arrived at the mountain cabin in the midst of the dark night, I lit a candle and meditated until dawn. I called for help to the Buddhas and the Bodhisattvas who it is rumored support earnest pilgrims on the path.

As I looked about the cabin, from a dusty bookshelf once again the right guidebooks appeared at just the right bend in the path.

In one, a Chinese fable told how each person must choose an animal spirit capable of supporting and conveying his or her constantly expanding spirit-body. Some use a bull or a workhorse, others an elephant, a whale, or even a dragon. Some of the most wily choose a fox.

But as I looked about in the woods and in my mind for the next few days for a suitable conveyance for my undernourished dharma body, only the small gray mouse hopping from sunspot to sunspot across the weathered wooden planks of the porch seemed to wholly comprehend the potential for boundless fear or boundless joy.

I took the mouse to heart.

The mouse suggested I open a recently received gift box from the Lama Foundation I had lugged along. In it was a copy of *Be Here Now* by my *Oracle* acquaintance Richard Alpert turned Ram Dass. It reminded me again that there was so much more to the world than pain.

Page after page cut old moorings and drew me out to sea, across the horizon through the great heart of Ram Dass and into the arms of his enormous teacher, Neem Karoli Baba, known affectionately and respectfully as Maharaji (often translated Great King or, better yet in this case, Great Spirit).

I heard deeper than ever before the Buddha saying, "You can look the whole world over and never find anyone more deserving of love than yourself."

Taking one breath at a time, I began to find my way. That which for so long had blocked my heart was breaking down.

Meeting with mercy and awareness, rather than continued suppression, those parts of myself lovely and otherwise, I was getting a teaching in opening my heart in hell.

I was learning to love by watching how unloving I had been.

I was so astonished and ashamed at my previous unconsciousness, I had to step back and take a breath.

As I opened my heart in hell, there was a letting go of the hard resistance to states such as fear. Noting it with the "Big surprise, fear again!" of gradual acceptance. The hard mind softening into mercy and awareness.

It is said the blood-soaked goddess Kali is transformed into the golden goddess Durga when we meet our fear with loving-kindness.

Indeed, it was this continual surrender and opening practice that allowed me throughout the experience, no matter how bad, small or how wonderful, big, the persistent feeling that I was doing this *with*, and perhaps if I could ever get this into words, even *for* all those who too were struggling to the surface. That perhaps there was in all this the possibility of a shared healing so great it bordered on liberation.

I was up a dark river, but not without a paddle.

The power of forgiveness was never so transcendent.

The hellish recriminations, confessions, and pleas for redemption melting at the edge. I began to float in something kinder and more spacious than small mind. In the midst of what seemed at times like hell I did not plead for forgiveness, but rather began to offer it. To the hungry ghost displacing the soul I sent concern for its well-being. I reminded the trembling ghost of the true light of its Great Nature obscured by its fear and its hell-solidifying self-judgment. The loss of natural empathy. The loss of Big Mind's generous perspective on small mind's density.

Each morning I went for a walk in the remarkable redwoods and sat by a small pond in a clearing a mile from the cabin. One day, beginning the forgiveness meditation, often practiced by Buddhists as part of the cultivation of loving-kindness, I turned to myself (an unfathomable mystery) and said, "May you be happy, may you be free from suffering," as I had hundreds of times before, but this time my body began to shake.

As I continued a bit bewildered I could feel the senses open. Something truer than grief was turning in toward itself with the compassion of the Buddha. Looking itself kindly in the eyes, it was like a long-lost friend. There was a sense of appropriateness and gratitude I had rarely experienced.

"May you, yes you, may you be free from suffering. May you be at peace!" I was trembling and began to weep. I had never known such room to be, such care for my well-being.

This great letting go of identification with my lowest sense of self, with my prideful self-rejection, sank deeper. Somewhere in the chest not far from the heart I could hear and physically feel a great door swing open. The bones in my chest, the seam in my sternum, made a loud pop. Tears of joy soaked my beard.

"May I be free from suffering. May I be at peace." The excited breath slowed. A warmth suffused my limbs, spreading through my body, and settled in my heart. There was absolute quiet where there had been fear and judgment.

My mind and body became as still as the surrounding forest. Sitting by the pond for perhaps an hour, I looked down to see a glistening salamander walk lazily across my sneaker. I was fascinated with the sun uniquely reflected off each muscular scale. It took her slowly undulating backbone an eon to cross my foot.

And something within, as though it had been forever hiding its countenance, turned toward me and said, "Stephen, I love you," and after a pause, "I forgive you."

It spoke of love in the voice I had been waiting my whole life to hear it in, my own voice. The only voice in which I might have believed it.

It was not until I heard that love in my own voice that I could wholly accept it from another. Indeed, it seems I could not truly love, or love truly, until I felt it at least to some degree for myself.

Until that moment I had not realized how much more there was to "love" than a state of mind. It was another defining moment in the coincidence of love and awareness. For the first time I had experienced in a place deeper than thought that love was an effortless and self-effulgent natural state of Being.

I recognized love as clear awareness, as consciousness freed from its self-constructed, self-flagellating prison. An absolute openness.

And Sujata when I told him of the recent strugglings and break-throughs said in nearly that same tone heard by the forest pond, "A day of facile forgiveness when the heart flows with ease is not the end but the beginning of the work to be done. Continue daily for a year or two no matter how awkward on occasion and see what shatters in the meantime. See what remains when confusion and self-loathing no longer obscure something too beautiful for words."

When I asked him how I could have this much love and still not be free, he said whatever I feared more than closing my heart would forever turn me away from my enlightenment.

And the healing that never ends continued. As I came to discover that the all-too-theatric imagery at the bottom of the underdream was, in fact, "nothing personal," just the repressed parts of millions of years of evolution in our frightening primal endowment.

When we meet with mercy and self-forgiveness rather than with continued suppression, all these aspects of ourselves, lovely and other-wise, we emerge a bit more born from this process.

And what had been taken so painfully personally and subject to, and of, so much judgment becomes simply the unfolding of a universal dynamic expressed in all-too-familiar terms. An invitation to mindfulness, kindness, and forgiveness.

On the rise out of the dark night, it was noted at dawn that, unrecognized at the time, many boundaries, which had been crossed on the descent, remained open on the way out.

I was a bit boundaryless and very much in love.

SEVENTEEN

forgiveness

The cultivation of loving-kindness made it increasingly clear that I could not let go of anything I did not accept.

Forgiveness finishes unfinished business.

"I ask the forgiveness of anyone or anything that I may have caused pain, intentionally or otherwise."

Forgiveness was essential to the uncovering of my original nature. It was a primary letting go of the hindrances to seeing, such as identification with self-congratulating pride and shaming self-judgment.

To let myself be forgiven was like sandblasting away my armor.

Somedays it exposed the heart for hours. Sometimes it didn't last to the end of the sitting. Sometimes I felt like I was wrestling with alligators. Somedays I was eaten alive in identification with the wound, trying too hard or not hard enough.

Sometimes, on a really good day, I floated side by side with my gator in an unexpectedly merciful universe.

"Just as I wish to be happy, so do all sentient beings. May they too forgive and be forgiven. May we all find our way home.

"I forgive whoever caused me pain intentionally or unintentionally.

"Just as I wish to be forgiven for the difficulties I may have caused, so I wish others to be forgiven, that we might put down the burdens of the past and enter anew the present, lighter and kinder."

Asking for forgiveness and offering forgiveness deepens our healing. It retrieves parts long buried and abandoned. It brings more of ourselves to the table. It offers more to that clarity of mind that only the word love seems to resemble. More to love and be loved.

When we forgive ourselves there is room now for another.

When we forgive others there is room then for the rest of the world.

Forgiveness gradually retrieves the heart. And with it a sense of all the hearts struggling at that moment to the surface.

Many Eastern teachers, including His Holiness the Dalai Lama, did not at first quite understand the Western preoccupation with shame. Many of our most compassionate counselors and therapists were focused on "working through shame." And rightfully so, considering the obstruction to clarity it presents and its magnetic, seductive ability to draw identification away from the heart. And it seems that a low, religious pedantry has coaxed an accompanying and all too available mercilessness into what some refer to as a "shame-based society."

This healing we receive, this continuation of our birth, as we delve into the mystery for a deeper glimpse of ourselves is clearly for the benefit of all. We work within to heal the guilt and self-loathing that, unexplored, so often leads to violence and abuse in a society.

When we start to take forgiveness practice seriously, the quality of guilt naturally calls for a mercy and softening that can soothe the involuntary arising of afflictive emotion. We learn to soften to mental pain just as we have discovered the remarkable power of softening to physical discomfort.

Interestingly, in the literature of Buddhist meditation what we call shame is not considered an unwholesome quality in the same way it is in the West. Shame is seen in the context of compassion and right action as a reminder of how far we can stray from the compassionate ground of being. Indeed, in the process of meeting our pain with mercy and awareness instead of fear and judgment, what we call guilt does not harden into shame, but instead softens into remorse. And a sense of being able to do it better next time.

Shame is an aspect of unhealthy negative attachment, while re-morse is a quality of a healthy conscience. From remorse arises a mind-fulness of the feelings of others and our capacity to meet even our own reactive anxiety with something kinder than judgment and fear. The potential of forgiveness is never so clearly demonstrated as when we begin to note such qualities as guilt with the lightness of "Big surprise, guilt again!" Same old, same old, met by something timeless and new. Met by the possibility of liberation.

In those moments of clear reflection when the ground of being becomes apparent, as Ondrea says, "There is who we are and the rest is what we've accumulated." There is the boundless ground of being, the space it's all happening in, the Deathless. And the rest is the personal-ity maze. We no longer mistake how we are for who we are. And for-giveness slips in between the cracks in the armor that imprisons us.

The Dalai Lama, in reinforcing our trust in our own great uninjured and uninjurable essence, reminds us again and again that under it all we are the One Light of Buddha Nature. That our true nature is enlightened goodness.

Indeed, a proof of this effortless natural goodness is demonstrated when people are not stressed, their hearts not obstructed: how natu-rally kind and remarkably beautiful they become.

Thus, meditation practice encourages us to recognize the difference between the actor and the action. To separate the doer from the doing.

One learns how to recognize, in others and ourselves, that being of pure awareness lost beneath a tangle of afflictive conditioning. In this practice one does not forgive or condone such things as cruelty, but may in time with practice begin to sense beneath that harmfulness a being whose true nature has been eclipsed by conflicting desire.

Indeed, that old saying "A person is only as good as his or her word" is not really true. Everyone is better than that.

In this opening of the mind to the heart one comes to understand that there really are no heartless beings, only heartless actions. In just this same way there are no enlightened beings either, just enlightened actions. Where there is *someone* to be enlightened, there is that same unwieldy someoneness to be ashamed.

To be in the world but not of it is to relate from the ground of being to the castles in air in which most live like ghosts. Haunted by self-image, we come to merciful awareness as to healing waters to be exorcised of our incessant self-consciousness. Floating in these healing waters, we look up from the pond to find no Narcissus looking back.

Many in the course of spiritual and psychological healing begin to share their relief and growing enthusiasm for the forgiveness meditations.

Surpassing the rational, and loving so accurately, they overflow with a sense of possibility and sometimes begin to teach their departed loved ones "on the other side" how to forgive themselves so they might be lightened for their next evolutionary leap. Forgiveness seems particularly useful for those who find unfinished business.

The practice exposes hidden layers of the mind to healing in an ongoing process.

Even as I write this, years after the experience by the pond in the redwoods, I notice my karmic bundle still has some loose ends hanging from it. A few loose threads, like an untied shoelace, to remind me to be mindful if I am not to get tripped up.

It took a while before forgiveness practices helped to resolve some of the personal grief of the long-conditioned, tight-boundaried, generally-identified-with small mind, or what we call "my mind." So it took a labor of consciousness before the unconditional openness of Big Mind would be able to relate wholeheartedly to the confusion of little mind.

Forgiveness cultivated Big Heart. Big Heart cultivated Big Mind.

EIGHTEEN

big mind liberation

Though I did not choose, as did Orpheus and Dante, to go into the shadow play of the underdream to retrieve the beautiful from the horrendous, it nonetheless happened.

As the investigative mind and the expanding heart allow us to approach "the unapproachable," we can look our self mercifully in the eye. And as we at last "take tea" with what some refer to as their "demons" and others recognize as their "fallen angels," we welcome even our pain into our heart. A heart that does not exclude even hell from its mercy.

As the process of the dark night unfolded and I was temporarily lost in the swamplands of the psyche searching unsuccessfully for some solid center, the mouse of faith on occasion broke through small mind into Big. And there rose from the heart a remembering of the wider perspective of Big Mind opening to encompass the whole. Relating from the awareness in which a frightened consciousness floats, clarity and compassion begin to open all about the grasping.

It was not a change in mental content. (That happens all by itself when we don't insist that our suffering is the only thing that is real.) But an opening in which thought and feeling unfolded in the vastness of clear awareness.

And the beautiful truth arose:

Most of our pain is due to lack of a deeper truth.
The opposite of pain is not pleasure, but clarity.

Viewing small mind from Big Mind, the personal from the universal, watching *my* mind from *the* mind can free us from the deepest and most pain-provoking of delusions.

Watching the tendency toward identification, which turns pain to suffering, attempting to reassert itself. Habitual mind-shrinking tendencies making themselves all the more real by trying to clutch "my suffering" to its dramatically aching breast.

The difference between watching painful inclinations with mercy and awareness and identifying with, and becoming them, is the difference between freedom and bondage.

When I observed during moments of clarity emotions such as fear received in mercy and awareness, it was clear that only identification in the form of resistance to that fear could cause me to become afraid.

It takes Big Mind, *the* mind, to observe without becoming lost in identification with small mind. And the space in which we can discover ourselves expands. The cramping too obvious to ignore, we let our pain go into *the* pain.

When it is *my* suffering, it can get unbearable. I am locked away in the dark night of my helplessness and confusion. When it is *the* suffering, I have room to breathe. I expand past the cramping around misery. When *my* pain becomes *the* pain, denial of the pain we all share ends, and true compassion begins.

Relating from small mind is to identify with each juggling act in the passing show. When anger passes through you become angry. When memory arises you are light-years from the present.

Small mind is a belief system: the erroneous concept that we are only the ordinary mind, the content, rather than the awareness from which consciousness is derived. Small mind is convinced everything is small. Big Mind doesn't even identify with the thought that it is big. It just watches thought arise and dissolve in the luminescence of awareness.

When a thought is related *to*, instead of related *from*, that thought is not identified with, but simply identified. Its content is acknowledged, even noted as such with "fearing, fearing." And perhaps eventually even met lightly with, "Big surprise, fear again!"

To relate *to* is to investigate, rather than invest, thought.

But we must be careful not to misuse so powerful a universe-reflecting tool.

We were concerned when we heard recently that some of the best Buddhist-oriented psychotherapists found that a few of the meditators seeking their counsel had to be redirected back to *my pain*, because the premature application of the *the pain* concept was abstracting their problem a bit and perhaps even putting it out of reach.

Of course, as in any healing, one cannot cover up the wound and not expect it to abscess. The looking at personal pain from a wider perspective comes slowly and in tandem with deep psychological healing that is mindful of tendencies to escape through denial and abstraction.

The merciful investigation of personal pain is the way to *the* pain before it becomes *my* suffering.

Big Mind starts small. Opening around the smaller, more easily related to thoughts and feelings, where identification isn't so much a reaction as an option. Working with what some call the "ten-pound weights," likening opening the mind to working out in a gymnasium. Don't grab at the five-hundred-pound weight to show from weakness how strong you are. You will just herniate yourself. As Milarepa said, "Hasten slowly." We can work out all day long with the little five-pound fears and desires we have learned so expertly to suppress.

To enter wholeheartedly even a ten-pound anxiety can provide considerable insight into the nature of fear itself. To expand into Big Mind is to take to heart all that small mind has gotten so skillful at suppressing. Mindful of the small fears and pains we have become so debilitatingly able to "control."

When we relate *to* consciousness, who we have come to fear and believe we are floats like a dream in the spaciousness of awareness.

Becoming aware we are dreaming while the dream continues, we become able to watch lucidly the dream evolve from moment to moment. Observing the unfolding with an open, even choiceless, awareness. No judgment, no clinging or condemning.

In these expanded states, when little mind floats in Big Mind, all that passes through is just passing show. Even the heaviest state has no effect, passing through with impunity.

Big Mind, in which float even afflictive states, is yet a greater peace than small mind walking the ramparts of its heaven always on the brink of holy war.

Small mind is hell. Big Mind requires no heaven.

NINETEEN

turning blue from not holding the breath

After I returned from the cabin in the redwoods and that two-month period of what Sujata classically called "the clarification of the heart by the uncovering of mind," he assayed my meditation practice. He said though he wasn't as impressed as I was with my moments of Big Mind, he felt if I had a bit more concentration I might be able to break through to the next level. He suggested a blue *kasina*.

A *kasina* is a round "meditation disk" into which one focuses, surrendering all transient thought and holding in order to reveal a deeper level of awareness. It has been used by forest monks for thousands of years to cultivate the concentration that gives strength of mind and steadiness of heart.

Use of the kasina is one of the Buddha's more than forty meditation techniques learned through yogic practice. Except for the simple brilliance of the mindfulness/insight practice, which it is said was the direct result of his enlightenment experience.

Kasinas are visual meditation objects into which one focuses uninterruptedly to reveal subtler levels of consciousness and more evident realms of awareness. It takes the wandering mind and, by repeated letting go of distraction and the reassertion of concentration, brings it to a profound focus. This is called *yantra meditation*. It uses visual images in the same manner that a mantra uses sound images.

YANTRA MEDITATION

An object of concentration and contemplation, a *yantra* is the visual equivalent of a mantra; it could be said the mantra uses the ears to the heart while the yantra uses its eyes. In Buddhist, Hindu, and yogic practices yantras often appear as sacred circles called *mandalas*, which range from the Tibetan circular maps of psychical realms to representational-as-symbolic overviews of heavens and hells and the states of mind and states of being that create them.

These circular yantras appear in most spiritual and religious practice. A peek through to the collective cortex perhaps. From the sand paintings of the Navajo to the floor mosaics and dome designs of many churches, synagogues, mosques, and cathedrals.

Yantric spiritual environments dedicate the heart to freeing the mind and give voice to the undeclared spirit.

In each yantra there is level after level of what could be interpreted as "meaning." But a yantra is much more than meaning. Much more than just the initial mirroring of our mental projections.

One does not simply look *at* a yantra, but *in* as far as one can, letting go of meaning and the pride of understanding to go yet farther.

One looks into a yantra as a means of seeing more deeply into the world around and within us.

In the beginning looking into a yantra can be like staring at a fire or gazing at a gaggle of passing clouds, formless thought projecting images into the ever changing forms. Learning by repeated letting go of superficial images to go deeper, we break beneath the surface world. It is like examining the surface of the mirror without being lost in discursive thought or distracted by your image staring back. It is a focusing through level after level of appearance until form breaks down and only its essence remains.

Sujata said I should make a blue kasina and work with it a few hours each day. He said it should be "a perfect circle the color of a deep summer sky."

Traditionally kasinas were constructed by meticulously pasting flower petals onto a twelve-to-fourteen-inch circular back piece, which was then concentrated on from a few feet away. To find just the appropriate blue flowers and place them in full color on the disk was in itself part of the commitment necessary for the hours of intense concentration the practice required.

But in the middle of the twentieth century I was told to get myself hence to a paint shop. And that it had to be exactly the right blue for it to work.

So began more than a month of paint stores visited and revisited and yet revisited once again, print shop maestros queried, and ink swatch samples looked at for "just the right blue." A dozen or more fourteen-inch art-board circles painstakingly made "perfect." Each receiving the etheric nuances between numerous shadings of summer-sky blue sprayed with the deepest and most even concentration. Each brought after a few more days for Sujata's approval and the opportunity "to get going" on this most fascinating practice. And week after week he said it wasn't quite right.

My frustration grew as it seemed, after numerous attempts and many hours of mindful work, that perhaps I was not going to get to do the practice after all because I just did not have "the eye for the job."

When I brought to Sujata what must have been the tenth meticulously painted circle, which I supposed he would summarily reject as "not having that ancient blue!" he glanced up for just a moment and said, "Yeah, that's it. Now get to work."

It was a lovely blue and served well, but whether it was "the blue" or not I have no idea. In fact it may have even been one I had shown him weeks before. Clearly I was being taught to stay one-pointed as part of my initiation into deeper levels of concentration.

Working with a blue kasina, one is instructed not to focus on concepts such as "concentration," or "meditation," or "round," or even "blue," but to "enter directly the experience of blue," which at the time sounded like a comic-book version of Zen, but since focusing one's attention for a length of time is known to intensify a sense of presence, I eagerly agreed.

I was not to think of blue, but only to let go of everything that blocked "blueness." It sounded weird and a bit woo-woo, but I trusted Sujata's insights. It was clear that deeper concentration was exactly what was required.

"And remember you are going for essential blueness only, nothing that makes sense, no idea, no enlightenment, just blue."

After about five weeks of working a few hours a day with "his precious blue kasina," I began to think Sujata had really missed the mark with this one. I felt barely concentrated at all. All that seemed to be "revealed" to me by this practice was how unconcentrated I was.

I could not stay on blue a millisecond before associated thoughts and hopeful self-inventories arose. Perhaps Sujata was just showing me how much work it really takes to cultivate awareness. Maybe this was a sneaky teaching in patience that my cruel and untrustworthy teacher had concocted to put me in my place. Of course on the way down and in, there is often a bit of paranoia to cut across. Who was this trickster who insisted on the impossible? A mind that was still? Never!!! How does one "Look straight ahead and not think about blue or round or dharma or concentration? When thought arises just let it go and return to blue once again"?

Not to think of blue, but to let go into that which is before it was called blue or color or round or even seeing.

Not to be someone experiencing blue, but just blue itself. No self-conscious meditator, no "getting healed," just blue. "Let go of everything but blue."

The focus returned a thousand times an hour to blue, for hours on blue.

Then a tiny glimpse of edgeless blueness. An egoless blueness immediately displaced by expectation and greed for more . . . Lost blueness . . . and back to the blue disk.

I thought I'd never *really* get it. And I noticed that thought float through between the inner eye of awareness and the absolute blue background. As the mind began to comment, returning my attention perhaps for the ten-thousandth time, I once again took the leap of faith into the centerless center of the blue kasina, no ground but blue, no one to be, nowhere to go, nothing to do. Its shining surface penetrated by a blue awareness.

And the mind stopped!!!

The last thought was gone, not as forever replaced by another . . . not even succeeded by a recognition that it had stopped, no mental action whatsoever . . . the absolute emptiness/silence that in retrospect made what I previously called peace seem like something of a nervous condition.

The silence within silence so complete not even a reflective thought, not even an experiencer, no "someone" rattling around in there, to acknowledge the experience . . . until thought once again resumed with a jolt, shaking the whole body.

That first thought ponderous as a locomotive pulling out of a rail-road station. A single thought like an earthquake in the silent vast-ness.

It was a nonexperience, which only became an experience/memory when that first thought recognized there had been no thought. A momentary cessation of consciousness.

Quite unexpectedly, it was not the stopping of the mind that caused the greatest of insights, but the opportunity to observe the mind reconstruct itself layer by layer, thought by thought, identity by identity, as it resumed operations.

One could see how completely true was the long-offered teaching that "Thoughts think themselves." The process continuing all by itself. I was simply the space in which it was unfolding, the awareness by which it was known.

For weeks after this experience/nonexperience warmth and patience suffused the body/mind. The mind was lost wandering in the heart observing in that endless clarity that what we have always been looking for is what is looking.

And no thought stronger than the gratitude I felt for the dharma, for the teachings, for Sujata, for blue, and even more for what lies beyond blue, altogether beyond blue, *Bodhi Swaha!*

A yantra is a meditation engine fueled by attention. The more concentrated the awareness, the higher the octane and the smoother it runs.

When the focus into an object becomes one-pointed, it is said the engine runs at maximum efficiency. There is neither friction from thinking nor the energy confusion of trying. It becomes like a perpetual motion machine whose momentum is increased by surrender. The essence of letting go that takes us closer to the living truth.

As one yantra practitioner said, "Place this engine near your heart and no matter what your vehicle, it will take you toward your destination."

After working with the kasina, the intensification of concentration greatly deepened my mindfulness practice.

As practice continued an hour or two a day, and included four or five two-week meditation retreats each year, awareness gradually became simply the ground of being.

In the course of developing a daily meditation practice, a year or so in, my body became so restless it could not sit still. With the mind more difficult to focus than usual, I went to Sujata to ask him the remedy. I expected him to say, "Take a break. You're trying too hard," as I had heard him say to others. But instead he said, "If you are having trouble sitting an hour, sit two hours." And it worked.

Some months later Sujata, hopeful of a comment for his new book, asked that I set up a meeting between him and Ram Dass.

Though through his book *Be Here Now* in the midst of my hard moment Ram Dass's presence had been a great aid, I had not seen him since the days of the Haight-Ashbury and the *San Francisco Oracle*.

Not wanting to take advantage of any slight acquaintance from a half-dozen years before, I suggested Sujata write Ram Dass himself. But he asked that I do it nonetheless.

Ram Dass wrote back warmly and said come ahead.

Reverently taking off our shoes downstairs, we were brought into Ram Dass's room. We sat on pillows on the floor, and I listened as he and Sujata conversed. It was not flowing. Sujata's unusually restless desiring was keeping them from connecting.

Quite unexpectedly, however, Ram Dass and I, eyes connecting, went deeply into a tunnel of light . . . no time, and what moves is forever still. I thought I might pass out, but with effort was able to "pull up in time," back into the body and the room and those eyes.

When we went downstairs to say our good-byes, there was a large black dog snarling on top of the shoe pile. Ram Dass warned us not to approach, as he had bitten recently. Everybody backed off.

In one of those moments when confusion gives way to the mystery, I trusted something strong within and knelt by the wrathful deity guarding the sacred mound of shoes. Reaching out a soft hand to the rigid dog, I touched his cheek. And he smiled, and we both resumed breathing as he leaned into the caress.

I have often thought that dog was just testing the password of my heart while creating a bit of theater to imprint the meeting.

Ram Dass suggested I visit again. And I did. We began working together on a book (*Grist for the Mill*). And eventually we began teaching together.

Sujata died of AIDS in the early '80s.

It is with profound gratitude that I bow to him.

A deep *gasho*, a deep *gasho*, a deep *gasho*.

TWENTY

becoming a *kalayana mita,* a spiritual friend

Meditating with fellow voyagers and spiritual friends, many of us in the mid-'70s increased the depth of mindfulness practice with the guidance of mindfulness meditation teachers Joseph Goldstein, Sharon Salzburg, and Jack Kornfield. Having published Sujata's and Mahasi Sayadaw's meditation instruction books, I offered to publish their teachings as well.

Editing Joseph's and Jack's first books for the Unity Press Mindfulness Series, meditating on certain paragraphs for several minutes at a time, permeated by their teachings, sometimes akin to "transmission," a direct transfer of wisdom from one consciousness to another occurred.

On my fourth two-week retreat with Jack and Joseph, perhaps a week or so into it, one evening in a very quiet moment I felt my gut release. It felt as though a fist long closed about my abdomen had opened. It was almost as though a hand that had reached down through the top of my head to take hold of my gut had withdrawn. Leaving me soft of belly and with a sense of physical and emotional freedom I had rarely known. It was more than just a physical unbinding.

It was more than just the hard relenting. What began as a physical release became a process of deeper and deeper levels of softening. Moment-to-moment softening, moment-to-moment letting go. A gradually expanding sense of freedom. Levels and levels of softening . . . the heart meeting with the disheartened . . . levels and levels of letting go . . . thoughts floating like bubbles in the vastness. "Nothing to do, no one to be, nowhere to go," as one teacher used to say. Nothing to obstruct the next level coming and going, no holding anywhere. Softening moment to moment, letting thought and feeling, memory and intention float in, rather than be grasped by, awareness.

Until that moment of release I never realized how rigidly my abdomen was being held. I was reminded of a fellow in one of the retreats I attended with the delightfully caped, highly skilled, European-born meditation teacher Ruth Dennison. He asked her what to do with the annoying ringing in his ears. When asked how long he had it, he answered, "Well, I guess I've had it all my whole life, but I just noticed it a few minutes ago!"

This gut-releasing experience was the basis for the soft-belly meditation that has been used by so many in so many ways at so many different levels: from those wishing release from a hell to those seeking access to the boundaryless spaciousness of heaven. It is particularly useful as a physical trigger for the mental state of letting go.

Softening from moment to moment, the hardening in the belly is seen to be directly connected to what is called the armoring over the heart. When the belly is softened, the heart begins to melt; there are waves of gratitude. The body opening . . . softening belly . . . opening heart . . . clearing mind . . . peace and that of which peace is an expression.

From this opening came a flood of insights.

After a few more years of practice, Jack suggested I teach meditation with the Insight Meditation group. In the southern Buddhist tradition the term for one who imparts the dharma is *kalayana mita,* a spiritual friend. When I asked why he chose me when there were so many others with decades more practice, he said, "Because of your life experience."

He gave me a copy of his lecture notes and sent a few tapes of his and Sharon's skillful-means interviews with students during long retreats.

I began teaching while learning further to serve those getting newly born and those completing that birth in prisons, hospitals, and meditation halls.

How much a slow, painful (to ourselves and others) rise through the realms of the hungry ghost can teach us. I could see with gratitude and appreciation how what now seems almost like someone else's life, what at times seemed unending confusion, could be transformed into clarity and compassion for the benefit of other sentient beings.

While editing Joseph's book, *Insight Meditation: A Natural Unfolding,* I asked if he thought I should offer meditation instruction at Soledad prison. Joseph said, "Probably."

Then I asked, "What should I say?"

Joseph simply replied, "When you get in that role, you'll know what to say."

I surrendered up a bit of my "not-enoughness" to take the teachings, which had been so lovingly provided to me, behind bars, where the truth is nowhere more called for.

It was a bit like the lama who insisted his students pray he be reborn in hell, "because that is where compassion and wisdom are most needed."

I wondered if I would ever be able to alleviate suffering and deepen understanding in the way my teachers had.

Like that time near the end of a long meditation retreat, when in the continuing course of opening to the new and clearing the old, the very ground on which I was learning to walk mindfully began to fall away beneath my feet.

In the midst of an immense moment in the ongoing process of rebirth, with one thought after another sliding off the blackboard of the mind, with old concepts peeling away like faded labels off rusted cans, all that I had known seemed so insufficient, so unreal.

With nothing solid and no history, hoping to find someone who could tell me if I existed or if this was a dream, I went to Sharon Salzberg.

She shrugged as deep as a bow and, raising an eyebrow, nodded affirmatively. And smiled and smiled and patted me on the head.

Standing before her in that kind of confusion that sometimes precedes a breakthrough, I asked, "What is real?"

Her warmth was like the sun coming out. Sharon's smile said it all: love was real.

I hope I have transmitted as much in my decades of teaching.

This transmission directly from heart to heart was clearly demonstrated when I was invited to teach with a much-respected influence on our practice, the holder of the Korean Buddhist lineage, Sueng Sahn. During the noon break, he ordered lunch for us in his private quarters.

Having a pleasant repast, speaking about nothing in particular, I realized I was wasting an incredible opportunity. And I asked quite abruptly, "Please teach me about koans." Koans are a Zen means of peeling back level after level of mind with a spiritual riddle that has no logical answer, only a suprarational intuitive one.

He smiled, said a few words about "no expectation" and "present only" and "just go straight," and offered the first conundrum.

I don't really recall all the words spoken during that remarkable hour, but I can still feel that sense of absolutely hilarious freedom. Something opened and we started popping koans one after another. And I could not stop laughing.

Whatever I had feared in "mysterious Zen" was now like a knock-knock joke, and there was nobody there. It was a most enjoyable experience.

Though I do not now remember all that was said, the quality of heart-to-heart transmission continued to display itself when I returned home in a rather rarefied state. On the three-hour drive home from the airport, I repeated much of the experience and Sueng Sahn's instructions to Ondrea. And she, who, like I, had seldom confronted a koan, began just as I had, after the first few awkward answerings, to levitate right through the process. In a matter of minutes the quality of clear mind imparted by our meeting was fully ensconced in her as well.

She experiencing the same uncovering of mind, and we laughed until our stomachs ached, popping koans all the way home.

This potential for startling clarity to be directly transmitted from one being to another, as Sueng Sahn had done with me continued on to Ondrea. Consciousness shared the unimpeded heart, the essence of spiritual friendship.

I went to the prisons and spent a little more than a year with a meditation group in Soledad prison while teaching my regular weekly classes in Santa Cruz.

TWENTY-ONE

death row:
an affirmation of life

After teaching in Soledad prison a bit more than a year, an expansion of this outreach seemed appropriate. I found myself working with men on death row in San Quentin and a few other prisons.

One of the warmest hearts I met during the years of working with the men on death row was the retiring warden of San Quentin prison.

When taping an interview for *Death Row: An Affirmation of Life*, he spoke in tones one might expect in a confessional booth as he told how he had been required by law to officiate at forty-five hangings during his more than twenty years as warden. The light in the room changing as he related details of a few of the executions he had attended. When it came to the hangings that "went wrong," his heart pounded like one who himself might be facing execution.

The death row book, like the men who had over the years worked to regain their souls and kindly participated, was as full of heart and insight as it was deep shadow.

In 1974 when the Supreme Court passed its ruling that capital punishment was unequally meted out and thus all death sentences must be reconsidered, most of the men on death row were placed back in the general prison population. Several were released because so much time under such horrific conditions had been served.

One fellow I had become quite close to acted as "inside editor" for the book.

Our visit together a few years later, just after his release from twelve years on death row, was as sweet and awkward and grateful and hopeful and filled with longing for life and God as almost any I have experienced. His wholehearted acceptance of his previous life and his long meditations on those he felt he had harmed had completed his unfinished business. In a very real manner of speaking, he completed that incarnation. Now he was like a newborn finding his earth legs.

He was one of the few people I have seen released from prison who was even close to being able to be called a free man.

He had eaten his shadow. Not all who were released at that time had quite so resolved their history.

The most spiritually inclined of the participants in the book was a tall pale fellow who had killed ten years before in a speed-crazed drug stupor. He said it took him three years to "awaken from the lethargy of prolonged drug use." He said he awoke to Vedanta: "I suddenly wanted to know the purpose of my existence, who and what I was as a conscious entity."

It was he who suggested that we end the book with a quote from Edwin Arnold's translation of the *Bhagavad Gita*:

Never the spirit was born;
The spirit shall cease to be never.
Never was time it was not;
End and beginning are dreams.

Birthless and deathless, and changeless,
Remaineth the spirit forever;
Death hath not touched it at all,
Dead though the house of it seems.

When he was released in 1975 he was met by a loved one whom he prayed to wed after they met some years before through a mutual attorney friend. He had an extraordinary job waiting for him as a highly paid legal secretary.

They got married; he was respected in the office; his home was warm and comfortable. But after a few months he started to become restless.

And a few months later he had a bad day. Like the guard's reply when we were leaving Oregon state prison after a "spiritual workshop" and we asked what one sensitive, open-faced nineteen-year-old with a wild Afro had done to deserve a ninety-year prison sentence: "He just had a bad day, a very bad day!" So too our friend had a very bad day.

After holding up a liquor store without incident, just as he was about to exit, he turned and for no apparent reason shot to death both of the employees standing behind the counter.

He is one of the very few people, perhaps the only person in U.S. penal history, ever to have been condemned to death row (four times faced a twenty-four-hour turnaround before a scheduled execution) who was released, then killed again, and had to be returned to death row for a second time.

Once again he has a date with death. And once again he will sit and rediscover his ever so fragile heart in hell.

When I first heard of his rearrest, I wondered what might become of the spirit of one so obviously attracted to spirituality, but so monstrously obstructed. Does he lose his spirit?

And the Unnamable Timelessness replied:

Birthless and deathless, and changeless,
Remaineth the spirit forever;

Death hath not touched it at all,
Dead though the house of it seems.

The FBI called some years later to ask if I knew the whereabouts of
one of the other contributors who had, from the row, been integrated
back into general prison population and later escaped.

I had not heard from him in years and told them so, but I could not
help imagining him on some beach in Acapulco or Sardinia reading
Gurdjieff and trying to figure out how he could have been so suicidal
thirty years before as to kill another.

And reborn, he wonders, "Was it I who did all that, but it wasn't
the same mind, and there was no mercy then. If I can ever fully forgive
myself, I might even be able to forgive my cruel childhood."

When asked by one of the men on the row what I might do if it
were me strapped into the gas chamber, I said "Hopefully, forgive."

Gandhi called out the name of God three times as he fell from an
assassin's bullets. He wasn't just having a good day. He had opened his
eyes to God each morning, so he was able to close his eyes with God
every night.

And could I, metering out the sort of lofty advice that gives rise so
readily to hypocrisy, be able to fill *my* last breath with love? Could I,
strapped in, as Maharaji taught, "Tell the truth, even if they stone you,
even if they crucify you, tell the truth"?

Months later, as I was transcribing the interview tapes at my desk,
my then-two-year-old daughter was playing at my feet. As the warden's
words filled the room with the image of the bloated and contorted face
of a "badly hung man," I abruptly turned off the tape and looked into
Tara's boundlessly innocent, deeply questioning eyes. The ironic juxta-
position of realms so painfully evident. This moment holding a two-

year-old's humming and drawing counterpointed by the revenge of the "civilized" family. It was a moment of world-weary, of time-weary, timeless compassion.

And how clear it became at that moment that the Divine and the wretched are equally sacred. That this life, this child's instant, this murderer's last moment, are all of a single piece. All united just below the fearful surface with a wish to simply find our way home.

Jesus was an outlaw, so they strapped him in. Way past go, enter directly your Father's House, your Mother's Boundless Garden. The murdered and the murderer perhaps enlightened over eons of reflection.

The stars in the Milky Way stretch between our mercy and our mercilessness, between our joy and our forgetfulness, between being fully born and never dying wholly into love.

In the lineage of Jesus and the Antichrist, of spirit and flesh, sitting at my desk, Tara now thirty-four with four children, and I heard they killed two more last week in Texas. But I'm told that now that we have begun to forgive even our Judas, it's not so easy to find someone to pull the switch anymore.

TWENTY-TWO

family healing

As my practice deepened, I would often go to visit my parents on the way back from long meditation retreats. I was very cooled out and quite in control. Precious as it was, nothing was gained but my parents' approval. We were not moving any obstacles. Posing as Buddha, I was not really growing much. So I instead began visiting on my way out to the meditation center. The work that was to be done presented itself. The agitation that called for mindfulness and mercy had its homework to complete.

Forgiveness begins at home. The home we left so long ago to find our true family. The home we return to when the heart has room for suffering as well as grace.

Later in the meditation hall, from beneath my meditation pillow the roots that sank into the earth drew on something closer to the molten core. Levels and levels of healing. Levels and levels of getting born.

A wonderful image used by Angelis Arrens to describe the possibilities and responsibilities of healing is from a tradition in which it is felt that over one's left shoulder is the long line of our ancestors on our mother's side and over the right are all our father's antecedents. All are watching hopefully and encouragingly saying, "Maybe you will be the one that breaks the family dysfunction."

As we grow and learn that quite to our surprise we are actually one of those sentient beings we have vowed to liberate, even more astounding is to discover that our odd family too is made up of sentient beings. The same category as those we have made a covenant to support in their emancipation from suffering.

On the night his son was born, Siddhartha left his home behind.

He named his son Rahula ("attachment/hindrance") and, turning wholly toward the mystery, put aside all that might distract him from his intended purpose.

He returned thirteen years later to take his son into the family business.

Much of course could be said of their relationship, but their case history is always best discovered in the Rahula within. The child who feels abandoned by God. The lost child, the Rahooligan, always unworthy, long turned away from the mystery. Inadequate.

I saw how none of that need get in the way for more than a few moments before the mystery infiltrates between thoughts and behind concepts and starts breaking down the glue that holds the illusion of separateness together.

When my father was in high school, he listened over earphones to the recently invented radio on a "crystal and whisker set" of his own making. Thomas Edison was his hero.

Our mind connection was strong particularly around an interest in science. When I was a child, he had helped me set up a small laboratory in our cellar. Feeding me cabinets, lab tables, a microscope, shelves of chemicals, lab glass, and his old chemistry books from college.

Our heart connection was something we both had to work on our whole lives until it finally came to bloom. But even now, years after his death, I notice in this writing hairline fractures in our façade, of the still-to-be-completed, of love still being exchanged.

In his last year of high school, the first year of World War I, he was selected by the military as an outstanding science student and given a scholarship to MIT. He had two years of intensive training in highly inorganic chemistry, focusing particularly on chemical warfare. On occasion when I would ask him about some fine point in a chemical reaction, he would say, "We never learned that; our education turned out to be pretty much focused on one thing." All they had taught him was how to kill large numbers of people in a most horrific manner.

It blinded his vision.

Living at times too long in this world, he carried his pain with a dignity from which I am still drawing strength.

Because I had been a bit of a difficulty for my parents in my youth, I wished for them to see the world in which I lived.

On one visit home such an occasion serendipitously arose. A physician friend who led the hospice program at St. Peter's hospital asked if I might give a short talk to some of the nurses and volunteers and perhaps a few others. It was coincidentally the last week of their hospice training program.

I said jokingly that I'd check with my mom to see if I could go out that night. And if I could, I'd bring her along. Although she had read some of my writing and an interview or two, she had never come to a talk.

After supper, leaving my father content with the *Wall Street Journal* and a large toxic cigar, we went off to the hospital meeting room.

Entering the room, we were both a bit surprised that so many people had been able to attend on such short notice. I looked over at my mother in the front row every once in a while, and there was light in her eyes. As the evening was nearing completion, I mentioned to the audience my delight at my mother's presence.

There was for her a quite unexpected round of applause. And before she could stand to leave, several from the audience came up to her, greeted her, and hugged her one after another. My mother was immersed in a swirl of love as perhaps never before.

On the way home, she was rather radiant and somewhat shaken by their "highly unusual warmth." With a mixture of bewilderment and pride she said, "They were so very nice," and as though scripted by Himself, "and a few even thanked me for you!"

With a bow and a wink to the Theater of the Heart just this side of the veil. The account at Karma Savings and Loan came a bit more into balance.

Sometimes I hear my brother's laugh in mine. We were never close as children, but now sometimes I feel his life inside mine.

Our father had a very large laugh. Our mother could find him in a crowd by his "great Bostonian cackle."

When we laughed at the dinner table, it may have been the closest our hearts came.

If we might have cried too at the dinner table, it may not have taken us all so long to cross the barriers to the heart.

But eventually I fell in love with my father. In time we even shared some slight mystical happenstance, which surprised us both and signaled that our path was straight ahead.

And the last time we were sitting together, he at ninety-one, I at fifty-four, Ondrea at forty-five, he dropped his head onto my shoulder and with a long, slow sigh surrendered up all that had ever kept us separate.

When he leaned over after breakfast a few weeks later and died, I could, and still, feel his head on my shoulder.

On the refrigerator one morning when this was a house coming and going with children, a few words from our oldest son, James:

Love this boy of storm-raw beauty.

The next week he turned twenty-one in his favorite old brown leather jacket, hair curling to his shoulders. Eyes soft as that well-worn leather, old pain like flecks of emerald in that deep mahogany. The wrestler's proud chin. The lover's broad shoulders. Hands of doubt and mercy.

In the mind's hero journey he flexes and smiles, covering all the bases just in case.

Born from himself, he emerges strong and gentle. Come to save all he loves from loneliness and the unexpected.

A warrior contemplating the end of war.

Another sweet coincidence is that our youngest son, Noah, now teaching meditation in Juvenile Hall and running the program for adolescents at Spirit Rock Meditation Center, and I are writing somewhat similar books at the same time. We read chapters to each other over the phone about passing through some of the same initiations from similar drives.

We are learning about each other even more. I hear how he survived his streets, he hears how I navigated mine. We wander along with a special appreciation for the dharma after having strayed so far and nearly gone over the edge before we could find the middle of the path. And sometimes I am his teacher and sometimes he is mine.

TWENTY-THREE

o and O and i

About twenty-five years ago, in 1979, guiding a week-long Conscious Living, Conscious Dying retreat at the Lama Foundation in northern New Mexico, I met Ondrea.

She had come for two reasons. First and foremost she attended to sharpen her already well-developed skills as a counselor and caregiver to the terminally ill. Second, she came perhaps to die (two past operations for cancer). Though, as she said later, she was looking more for advice on the former than the latter issue. "Death I know; compassion I am still learning."

As the group began the Sufi dance that closed the weekend retreat at Lama, Ondrea and I were quite surprised at our energy together.

I recognized her immediately.

I had been looking for her my whole life in everyone I met.

When it was signaled to change partners in the dance rondo, we did not separate but eddied off to one side. We have been together ever since.

And turning, turning, turning, we were married in that same building, nearly on that same spot, a year later.

It is most noticeable in my version of pilgrim's progress that little is said about my relationships until I met Ondrea. I was married twice before I committed so fully to our union. As I said, my first wife and I were perfectly off-kilter together. My second wife and I were not made for each other. We could not even agree on how long it took to cook a three-minute egg. We are still friends. I am the godfather of one of her subsequent children.

Ondrea and I have accumulated three children and four grandchildren. And I thought before their births I knew what service was! Well, the mystery certainly amended that. There is no selfless service quite like that of having children. Indeed, the difference between selfless service and thankless service is well explored in this environment.

Considerable progress has been made on the shared path with Ondrea during these past twenty-five years of interbeing and support. Certainly our process together has been reinforced by the care and surrender that were required during the aftermath of her cancer and later immune disease. That love and surrender did as much to draw the mind into the heart as any practice I have ever undertaken.

We can make a thousand vows, but all we truly have to offer each other is our heart.

We travel alone our whole lives. It is such grace to share that loneliness with one we love.

To trust and be trusted, to love and be loved.

We are each a cell in the body of humanity. Out of the immensity we find each other and create a new life. This new life is in our eyes and in our bones.

When two share the One, the heavens rejoice that these two continue the lineage that began even before they recognized Eden in each other's eyes.

One teacher said make your breath your best friend. Another said your only friend is God. For me, her breath is God and the sacred would be less accessible without it.

A Zen Master friend used to sign his letters, "Please get enlightened and free us all."

We wed with that intent to stop nowhere, to treasure the living truth even more than each other. And to treasure each other beyond measure.

4:00 A.M.

Ondrea waking sat in meditation

Buddha recommended meditation
in "the third watch of the night"
in that stillness, in that darkness
the light becomes most intense

at the dark window numberless faces
dissolve one into the wretched next
in crowds that push forward
for her blessing
and each gets what they came for
an open heart attracts the penitent
from other worlds

Sometimes stamens singing in deep-throated flowers chorus with the wind, her beloved wind, to remind me once again that only she and the mystery are real.

I may bow in all the six directions, but I am always only bowing to you and You.

A knotted Kleenex left
beside the meditation pillow
submerges me in you.

TWENTY-FOUR

attending

I was teaching a retreat with Ram Dass in 1976 when I met Elisabeth Kübler-Ross. After an afternoon's meditation, she invited me to attend one of her five-day workshops.

At her workshops a calling to serve the dying arose. She invited me to a few more, and I decided to ask if I might offer meditation teachings for caregivers with her.

Soon after, while she was visiting California, during a day of repeated near misses we connected, and when I asked her what she felt about the possibility of my teaching with her, she said without hesitation, "Well, if it feels right to you and it feels right to me, then it must be right!"

When I was first teaching with Elisabeth, I appreciated again and again hearing her say, "Nothing is too good to be true!" It gave me a sense of unlimited possibility. It helped me find the light whose blockage we call shadow. It authenticated the miracle of our potential.

I worked with her for a few years. She initiated me into the joy and heartbreak of working with the terminally ill in a hospital room in Houston, guiding me into the only chair beside a dying young woman's bed and retreating silently into the corner.

There was nothing I could say that felt right. All my "methods" were obstacles to our connecting. I sat quietly next to her for a while, then picked up her hand and let our breaths find their natural rhythm together. Softening, she said she was tired of fighting death, so many operations, so many "last ditch" experimentals.

I said that with her remarkable heart death would not be a problem. And she said she knew.

Exhausted as she was, it seemed she was blessing me. There was a quality to the shared silence that I have only known in the meditation hall.

I do not remember all that was said, but I do remember the heart-joining silence and our breath and the nearly overwhelming ocean of compassion on which the scene was floating. And the words, less faint all the time, that rose in my heart from some distant memory of the Native American tradition, "One heart, all same!"

It was perhaps that so much helplessness could coexist with so much trust in the process that I was drawn toward this work.

Nothing is too good to be true.

My heart was beckoned as the dying became my teacher and path.

When I met Ondrea, I was running the Hanuman Foundation Dying Project. Ram Dass suggested we maintain a free consultation phone for the dying and their loved ones. We did so for three years.

Our work with the dying over these more than twenty years has been a great gift to us. It has been our path with a heart.

Sitting up with Jennie, we check the clock. It's 2:57 A.M. in New Mexico, 4:57 in Philadelphia, where Jennie seems to be in the process of dying, and Dan is close at hand.

We have sat so many death watches. But Jennie and Dan are nearly a continent away. So we sit at home holding them in our heart.

Jennie had been ill for a long time, but now the end was in sight.

She wrote, "We've decided on depth, not breadth." And opted out of what she found to be very consciousness dulling procedures.

"Everything is becoming more simplified. She feels the chemo is so queer and invasive that it obstructs her touch with herself, with her natural process," wrote Dan. He continued:

> *So now comes Jennie to this moment. This turning in the road we always knew, this turnout place.*
>
> *Where grief has always sat now comes the immense, unmapped, untamable, unfathomable, unmitigated, undomesticated, never-explored UNGHH of grief, the thing itself, curdling everything.*
>
> *Jennie, whose great muscle to explore, unravel and open to rising illness has been year by year so astonishing to live beside. Now she seeks around a certain Endgame the edges of gratitude and peace. . . . The courage to turn her healing toward death.*

In meditation there repeatedly arises the image of Jennie holding a small candle. She is leading others through mottled shadow down a path that disappears over a bright horizon.

Animals loved her and water leaned slightly toward her when she passed. Love creates tides. She was the moon. Her power was in reflection. Her mind opened like a crystal array behind the simple candle of her heart, converting its light to art and healing.

They know the patience that surpasses understanding. They have what love bestows when we most need it.

A few days later, passing through, Jennie said to Ondrea, "This is just so wonderful. You're going to just love it when you get here."

And the candle went out and filled the room with light.

The residential Conscious Living, Conscious Dying retreats and workshops we offered for twenty years were generally attended by a few hundred people.

Though I have shared many "miracle" dying stories over the years in such books as *Who Dies?* not all our work was so clever, clear, or theatrical.

On one occasion a fellow with a brain tumor with whom I had been working for about a year came for what he called his "last retreat." The growth of his tumor had displaced most of his life. He might have a few "good hours" in a day, and he asked if I would spend time with him in his cabin as he was too weak to attend in the main hall.

He was a particularly gentle soul. Very tall and now quite thin, he said he was going to be a Giacometti sculpture in his next life. I loved him a lot and of course wanted his impending death to be as gentle and fulfilling as the hours we spent together.

One afternoon after a somewhat shortened visit due to pain, I reminded him if it got too bad and he needed whatever help I might provide to come wake me, no matter the hour.

At 3:00 A.M. he came to my room weeping with pain. The medication wasn't covering it. Could I just give him "some energy"? Often I had put my hands on his head during guided meditations. Our connection was palpable in a subtle flow of electrical energy through our touch. He said it soothed him.

But this night for some reason I could not fully wake up. I was in an unshakable daze. Because during these intensive events we work from 6:00 A.M. until sometimes hours after midnight, sleep offers a major recharging. And this night something in mid-charge was not unhooking sufficiently to interact with the world.

He lay down on the bed, and I sat next to him with one hand on his brow and the other over his heart. I began a guided pain meditation, but it was not at all as it needed to be. I could not wake up enough to muster the presence necessary to focus. I was a lump. My words, like my touch, were energyless. And his pain, rather than being soothed, was intensified by the walk to my room. He lay there half moaning, half singing to himself until more medication at last took effect.

It was a disappointment to both of us that I could not have been of more assistance. But it was a powerful reminder of what it means to those around us when we are half present.

Unable to focus with any depth, what I found most disconcerting was that when I touched him I couldn't feel him. I was ankle-deep in a very shallow consciousness. It was a remembrance of what it was like before I woke up. How isolated the heart was, how half lived my life.

For years in the San Francisco workshops, it was a running joke that Joanne was our bodyguard. Although we would often wink at each other when someone would kid about it, I pity anyone who might have attempted to do us harm in her presence. She was very big and very beautiful, like an African chieftain.

But her body was collapsing around her. And though her life mate, Cheryl, cared for her tirelessly when she was ill and played deeply with her the rest of the time, gravity was incessantly drawing her back into the earth.

Having outlived her bleak prognosis by almost three years, Joanne suffered in the last months the severe bodily disintegration of one who has stayed to the very last, "for love, not for the body," through a profoundly degenerative disease. Her bones actually breaking under the weight of her great body, her organs disintegrating within her. Her beloved Cheryl always at her side.

When she died, their two-year-old daughter said, "Big fish is dead!" Joanne loved to fish with her daughter. She loved most her dear Cheryl, who cared for her with an almost magical sensitivity and a level of exertion that knew no seventh day to rest. Who "held the light" for Joanne when she became so agitated and enraged at death a week or so before she died, "so she could find her way home."

Who held her to her heart as Joanne shook loose the early nightmares of her life review, detoxing from life as a gradually expanding sense of nonresistance and even ease allowed her to die her own death in her beloved's arms.

Before I met Ondrea, I worked with patients in the mid-'70s at times accompanied by, or accompanying, a tough, compassionate Dominican nun. Sister P. had a raucous laugh and a deep love of family. And no one was excluded.

One day she said because I had shared Buddhist meditation with her with such profound results (she had a series of insight experiences during our Tuesday night group sitting), she wished to share with me a practice of great import to her.

She took her Jewish Buddhist buddy off to the cathedral for a bit of wine and crackers. Taking me "backstage," she introduced me to the bishop. When she asked warmly, he gave permission for me to take the Eucharist in the service that was about to begin.

Though I had attended several Catholic Masses over the years after the death of patients, coming forward for a consecrated blessing was a new experience altogether.

When I knelt and parted my lips for the Body of Christ, I felt two wafers on my tongue. I was somehow being doubled up on blessing. And His blood dissolved the two into the One.

I figured the bishop thought I probably could use all the help I could get. And genuflecting there with my mouth full of spirit and flesh, I thought, "Don't get too rational with the Divine, or you'll miss all the detail!" And Jesus laughed, adding, "Don't look a gift horse in the mouth."

It was another moment with Jesus the Mystic, who I met through the influence of my Jewish Hindu teacher years before.

Many times I have bowed to Jesus with gratitude, because among the dying in this country he is often experienced as the archetype of the heart. A model for dying. It has been said in fact that because of our intrinsic longing for the Great Heart, even if Jesus never existed, the Jesus archetype would continue.

It has always struck me as bizarre that this being, whose love was so strong that it is still spoken of, should be represented so much more often as tortured on the cross than as the sacred heart. Exposing the world to a love that could have saved those tens of thousands of children who suffered and starved today.

He resides in that same place in my heart as does Maharaji Neem Karoli. Perhaps all great spiritual beings are just the pure emanation of that one soul we all share, the one we call the One.

I have never seen Jesus up close in a cathedral, but I found him once on my meditation cushion (please see Jesus in the Glossary) when I returned home late at night from the hospital. He put his arm around me and we wept for the patient's hard death.

Long before she killed herself, I walked with Antonia when she first stumbled and fell. "A.L.S.," she sighed and wept.

"Tony's dead and there's no one to help me like I helped him!"

And years later, as I told her story to three hundred AIDS patients, we gathered together in her helplessness and love and with her stumbled forward toward our own unknown with a bit more mercy. Weeping that so many die alone and that so much love goes unshared.

AIDS

Ondrea and I had sat bedside with the dying for some years before our first experience with AIDS in the late '70s.

Then one after another of some of the youngest and most beautiful patients we had ever worked with started coming to workshops and calling for assistance. There were workshops, particularly in California to begin with, in which there were two to three hundred people working with the virus.

Adrian, dying of AIDS, said, "I've always been an optimist, but that doesn't seem to be helping my body anymore. Now to be an optimist is to know I'm not that body." By this time he had to take a transfusion just to come to the weekend workshop. "I was just a quart low!"

"And, you know, I've thought a lot about why, if we are not the body, we have such a strong attachment to it . . . and I think I see mercy even in that very troublesome condition. . . . If we did not have that attachment, we might have killed ourselves long ago. . . . Even in the most difficult of times we have an intense, even irrational, desire to continue living."

He said he only had two questions before he could let go. "What will become of 'Adrian' after I die? Will I lose the personality, will I no longer be myself?"

To which Ondrea replied, "You'll be more yourself than ever! There will still be that sense of being, but it will have a considerably larger frame of reference than it has now."

His other question was whether taking medication for his sometimes piercing pain was somehow "unspiritual." And we replied that if the pain blocked his view of spirit, if it filled his body and mind so he could not get beyond the aversion and sense of helplessness, he should act toward himself as he would toward his only child. He should hold himself in his arms and give to the pain all the love and surcease (chemical or otherwise) it needed.

Imagining one must die with the body contracted in pain, hardened against life, unable to hear within its deepest song and prayer, seems less supportive of the spirit than a slight chemical veil that may be quickly passed through. The unstoppable momentum of the spirit passes through so many moments of unveiling on the way toward essential clarity.

He was luminous and died alone enfolded in the arms of his deep-seated image of the Divine Mother, what he used to call Mother of Us All.

As with attempting to protect "holy ground" at the wildlife sanctuary, there arose during this work with AIDS patients a certain almost political quality of social activism that sought to diminish the influence of those seen as destructive. Many in the service of AIDS patients found that a bit of the role of social conscience advocate presented itself.

A frozen few said AIDS was God's punishment, an old friend or two no longer hugged, and the ghetto walls were heightened. But there were angels everywhere to disperse the poison gasses. Angel-hearted physicians like Carl Simonton kissed the most self-conscious AIDS patients when they parted and reminded them of how deeply beautiful they were. The venerable physician Fred Schwartz devotes his life to heading the medical heart of the New York hospice. There was Trevor Hawkins, an M.D. in Santa Fe, who, like hundreds of other physicians, simply could not hold back. And the outstanding work of Martha Freebairn-Smith and Frank Ostaseski of the San Francisco Zen hospice.

"And what if you catch the virus?" I asked a deeply committed health-care worker in the first years of unknowing and love.

To which she replied, "They are so young and, for some, even their families won't come near. I can't let them die alone."

In those days, in which one could almost smell witches being burned, the plague was upon us. But it was not the virus—it was fear.

I am uncertain which fear was manifest the most. Was it fear of dying? Or the shades of a misogyny that passes for homophobia, the male fear of being womanlike?

It is clear upon examination culturally, socially, and/or psychologically that the fear and hate projected by some "straight" men toward gay men is an underlying fear of women and womanliness. In fact, it appears that the greater the homophobia, the less likely a man is to have a trusting, noncritical relationship with the opposite sex.

Ironically, in the face of this fear and ignorance, the gay community, the brotherhood of homosexual men most actively affected by the virus, became perhaps the most rapidly evolving spiritual community in the country. No other group seemed to be moving so rapidly from common closedness to extraordinary openness. No ashram or monastery had as many hearts opened, as many "lids lifted," as much overhanging luminescence, as did the Castro or the West Village.

How perfectly serendipitous that it was the way gay males were conducting themselves during this plague that set such a strong example for a weakening culture. Indeed, gay men were teaching us (mostly heterosexuals) "how to be a man."

At the heart of the AIDS community lay another grace. Those least susceptible, the lesbian community, entered energetically and respectfully to support their brothers and share the pain. Placing themselves squarely in what might have been harm's way. Part of the lineage of strong and merciful women and men found on every battlefield, whose love is so much greater than their fear.

In 1983 after *Psychology Today* published a long interview with Ondrea and me about our work with the twenty-four-hour "dying phone," we received eight hundred phone calls and three thousand letters. It took us nearly six months to attempt to fulfill the immediate need. Some of these relationships continuing for years afterward.

HEART OF THE WOMB

Just as the dying work had expanded and deepened with AIDS, so the grief work deepened and expanded when, in the course of a ten-day Conscious Living, Conscious Dying retreat, exploring the grief we all share, it became quite evident that many of the women in the room experienced a profound grief that did not result from the death of a loved one. They grieved the loss of trust and comfort resulting from sexual abuse.

After a particularly intense meditation, one woman stood up to share gleefully with the group her out-of-body experience during the meditation. Though that is not the intention of the practice, occasionally such experiences spontaneously occur. She was glowing with her discovery of being more than the body, of floating free from its denseness, when another woman somewhat anxiously raised her hand and said, "I don't mean to interrupt, but I have something very important to say." She stood. "You know, I think all this out-of-body stuff is real nice, real showy, but I'd like an in-the-body experience for a change. I would like my body to be a safe place to be, not a target. I would like my body to be home, but I never feel at home in my body because my body has been trespassed, vandalized. I've locked all the doors and now I can't get back in." Many women in the room began to sob, acknowledging the shared truth that the body was simply not a safe place to be.

After this very intense and incredibly moving session, a woman approached me and said, "You know, I have no more room in my heart now than I had in my body when I was two years old and my father raped me."

And it became immediately clear that women have two hearts, the heart in the chest and the heart in the womb. There was a powerful connection between the upper heart and the lower heart ("lower" is not used here in any disparaging sense, only as an anatomical designation). Many woman had found access to the upper heart difficult because of the necessity to close the lower heart, the womb, the genitals, for self-protection, for survival. From abuse to the womb there arose a fear, distrust, anger, doubt, even merciless self-hatred, all of which had limited access to the spaciousness and ease residing eternally in the upper heart.

And what I knew of grief painfully expanded.

Back in our cabin on the lunch break that followed that mind-bending exchange, the shared pain broke our heart. Our stunned silence expanded into a long loving-kindness meditation. And though we were momentarily overwhelmed by the suffering, we returned to the meeting hall ready to learn what might be done for the healing that was called for.

From this woman's words the *Opening the Heart of the Womb Meditation* (Sounds True Recordings) arose as if from grace. It allowed us to participate in the healing for which we must all take responsibility. None of us is separate from the pain that any of us carry.

Working all these years with adults who had been abused as children was in some ways more challenging than being with the dying. I had seen wonders and grace around the deathbed. But around abuse I found a yet more arduous healing. A struggling to be safely born. A great fatigue of the heart. But over the years we saw so many blessed in the opening into a new life. And we were deeply honored to take together with a few their first breaths as we had previously shared with so many their last.

Grateful to participate in healing dialogues "that clear broke open heaven" and allowed us each to see the miracle of the shared heart very much intact.

The greatest healing is the one we cannot but share.

TWENTY-FIVE

in the service of
the art of advocacy

Service often includes an element of advocacy for "right action."

WHAT IS NOT

The high end of most contemplative practices, and Buddhist ones in particular, encourages the exploration of *what is*.

We are encouraged to relate to the flow of change, to the ways of our world with kindness and forbearance. We are urged to examine the mechanistic quality of mind, its habits and reactions, as well as the deeply terraced holy lands within, its living suchness and responses, with equal respect, mercy, and awareness.

To see *what is* brings insight and a greater sense of detail and change, a sense of participating in what is viewed. To relate to *what is not* brings disappointment and disquiet.

So often the mind is noticed criticizing whatever it comes across. Everything is too big or too small, too much more like that than this and vice versa. Judgment entangles the senses.

Often upon encountering an object or situation the mind/mouth will address its weakness, its incompleteness, its failings. We speak of *what it's not*, instead of *what it is*.

We relate to *what is not* there, rather than experiencing *what is*.

After years of searching for a piece of land, in 1986 when our youngest child sailed off into the world, we found a beautiful parcel of forest and pasture studded with towering rock formations in northern New Mexico. It was just right.

Surrounded by tribal lands and the Carson National Forest, unfenced since the original homesteader was granted ownership in papers signed by Abraham Lincoln, there were here and there the stumps of great ponderosa pines and two-hundred-year-old pinyon pines cut by local woodsmen over the years. It was evident as we walked through the woods that some of those who came before us had very little respect for the land. Great trees cut years before but never bucked up into logs were left rotting. Senseless waste, the consequence of imagined dominion over the earth.

And we began to notice as we explored the land that even in the midst of a glorious stand of trees, we were often lamenting the stump of a grandfather ponderosa. We were talking about what was not there. We were not seeing the forest for that absent tree. We were in the midst of it all, relating to what was not there. Missing the mark. Another enlightenment down the drain!

How ironic to be unable to see what is right in front of you because of what is not in front of you.

Now certainly you might ask, what about injustices? Are we not to be concerned about the necessities of life that so many are being deprived of? What about hoarding in the midst of famine? What about genocide?

These are very tricky questions, for as many historians, including Joseph Campbell, point out, many Asian despots welcomed, even supported, Buddhism because it made the populace more accepting and easier to manipulate and abuse.

Are we not to stand up and say what is not? No medicine, no food, no housing, no peace, no safety, no freedom of religion, no ownership of our own bodies, no respect for the earth, no mercy.

The advocacy for the well-being of others, which nonetheless decries the use of harmful means, says, "Yes, stand up! Speak to what is not from a strong sense of what is, a sense of possibility!"

We are in training to see beyond what we see.

Beyond preference and our great-grandfather's models still in the topography of our mind, there is work to be done. Beyond our attachment to maintaining, even more than comprehending, what is, is the truth of what is not.

And beyond such dualities yet a greater truth: the heart that recognizes such suffering and acts to relieve it.

Is our heart half empty or half full?
Fill the void with service and tithing
and educational programs.
Build a house with Jimmy.
Visit the frightened, the elderly, the ill.
Be a mentor, remind each other of our true nature,
and in particular honor others. . . .
Do not say only what you fear they are not, see their Great Nature.
See the clutter from which unwholesome actions arise,
and don't mistake it for the luminous vastness that is momentarily obscured.
Each generation outdoes the last, let yourself be outdone.
Enter deeply what ever reminds you
that you are part of the mystery, everything present, nothing absent.

TWENTY-SIX

right action in action

"It's not hard to do good; it's just hard to do good well."

Right action is one of the practices of the Buddha's Eightfold Path to liberation. It means meditate and be kind. As another of these covenants, right speech, endeavors to speak for the benefit of others, so right action is action directed toward the benefit of others: peace-making, service, and caregiving. In this context it is the alleviation of suffering as demonstrated by the support of the weakest among us. The most disenfranchised in every realm from ghost and animal, through human, and even empathy for the gods that they couldn't go further.

In 1967, studying *satyagraha*, the art and spirit of living in a non-injurious manner, including nonviolent opposition to injustice, with Chinmayananda, who was one of Gandhi's lieutenants in the '40s, I was taught to draw outside the lines. When the audience asked him what he, with his view of all life, would do about the proliferation of rats in India, it expected a reply perhaps about every creature having its place in the scheme of things. Perhaps about increasing the number of temples where rats are fed and even worshiped as the god-serving rodents of certain Hindu holy books. But instead he said, "Get rid of every single one of them; they're taking food out of the mouths of starving children!"

Later that year Allen Cohen, my partner editing the *San Francisco Oracle,* and I marched on the Pentagon together with a few tens of thousands of others.

We were among the first to enter the Pentagon grounds, and we headed up the wide granite steps until stopped by a phalanx of soldiers, behind which stood a number of dark-suited federal marshals with three-foot-long riot clubs. Sitting at the feet of the military we took out our five metal Tibetan chimes and began to chant an exorcism of the Pentagon as billed.

"Gate' Gate' para gate' para sam gate' bodhi swaha!" ("Gone, gone, beyond gone, absolutely beyond gone, enlightenment hail!") we chanted to the punctuation of the finger cymbals. The marshals glaring down at us from just behind the line of young soldiers, slapping their riot batons against their legs in frustration and anger. The deeper the chant, the greater their zeal. In brutal self-flagellation they beat at their legs in time with the chant. We had to stop what had begun as a bit of exorcism theater out of concern for the well-being of the demons. They were probably noticeably bruised the next day and still a little numb at heart.

I have long admired the term "together action" because it describes so simply a multileveled healing process that begins when we address the mind from the heart. When we enter pain with mercy and awareness rather than withdraw from it in fear and judgment, we sense another level of togetherness in which our own pains are the pains of us all. In which our wish to be free, to be happy, is the universal calling. And we join in a commitment to the mutual healing of us all, as in the bodhisattva vow, where we let loose of even personal spiritual ambitions to stay available to the suffering we all share.

Together action is the combining of wills to build a home or lay a road, to stop a war or heal a culture, and often to move a large object of conscience.

As social activists we must be careful, when exorcising demons, not to push away some part of ourselves that is crying out for attention and healing. Or become what we oppose.

We must be watchful of narcissistic anger if we are to remain balanced in the midst of attached concern for another's well-being.

The Dalai Lama, Gandhi, Martin Luther King Jr., and Desmond Tutu point out that it takes more than a sense of injustice and the righteous anger that often accompanies it to fight "the good fight"; it takes peace.

Even though we may comprehend the cause of suffering—even how pain can become suffering—there can remain beneath it all the righteous anger of the hungry ghost.

Gandhi reminds us our resistance needs not be passive, only nonviolent. In any act of resistance we must remain vigilant of the difference between aggressive protection of those in need and the quality of hostility that may arise from the impotent rage that lies uninvestigated beneath the level of awareness. A latency that can obscure the heart's intuition for healing solutions.

If service includes an attempt to correct perceived inequities, we must be very mindful of our methods because all reformers are angry.

I know this all too well in myself.

As the Dalai Lama said, "It is better to skillfully express the pain before it turns to suffering and erupts as hostility. To bring forth world peace there must be mental peace."

An example of my reacting more than responding occurred some decades ago when I was publicly judgmental of what I perceived to be the general lack of focus in my beloved Buddhism on issues such as traumatic abuse. There seemed some confusion around concepts about karma, which smelled of old fears of Judgment Day, as saying that anything "bad" that happens to us is only of our own making, even perhaps a sort of punishment for previous actions. A very toxic and unskillful, all too shallow interpretation of a much subtler process. A misinterpretation that can be very injurious to victims of war, violent crime, and sexual abuse who need first and foremost to recognize that their ordeal was of another's making, another's intention, not their fault. Mindful that we don't end up blaming the victim.

I pushed for change, perhaps even distancing a few old friends.

As the number of AIDS patients increased, relationships were frayed with a few secretly gay meditation teachers who I privately challenged to speak up for the benefit of their students with AIDS. To perhaps offer more support to those raised in shame-based Western religions.

Or I, hard-bellied, listening to an honored Indian teacher saying to a frightened women that it was her duty to take care of her aging parents even though they had molested her for years as a child.

"Bullshit!" whispered my karmic bundle.

"Though excellent candidates, if and when the time is right, for long-distance loving-kindness and even forgiveness meditations," it softly added.

In the decades since those early confrontations, movements like Engaged Buddhism and the Buddhist Peace Fellowship, and an increased appreciation for the depths of healing to be done, have helped break down some of the superstition and cultural prejudices that are bound to be transmitted along with any millennium-old belief system.

The ideal balance for service seems to see from deep enough inside far enough into what's needed outside. Though as Suzuki Roshi might add, when service truly flows there is "no inside, no outside."

TWENTY-SEVEN

nuclear winds

Fifty-five years ago in Hiroshima we perfected hell, though we still never stop attempting to make it worse.

Burning the flesh off skeletons was not enough. We needed to melt the molecules of bone and brain alike.

And Ondrea and I wondered what it must be like to be vaporized by an atomic blast.

Would there be any pain, or would it happen so suddenly there might only be time for one last thought that hung in the air a moment after the thinker disappeared?

And now, in May 2000 in northern New Mexico, Los Alamos is burning.

We live thirty miles downwind from the end of the world, our bodies appropriated by science and the pinion breezes that bring life and death down the canyon.

At 7,200 feet the soft wind that carries bird song and pine waft and the stillness that surrounds great rock outcroppings carries perhaps a molecule or two toxic for a million years.

In the heart of the Carson National Forest in a home we built at the end of a three-mile dirt road that passes through tribal lands to the south, we live immersed in our process with few visitors other than our family and a few old friends.

Today as thick ash falls we are each and all one under the mushroom cloud.

White ash falling on the house. The black cat dappled with gray. Sun through high smoke drift casts a preternatural golden light.

Last night the moon was an orange slice.

The snow-peaked Sangre de Cristo (Blood of Christ) Mountains obscured as though seen through a white silk *kata*.

The bees have abandoned the apple blossoms.

They never returned.

They called it Los Alamos, which means "the trees," because it was on a high plateau surrounded by deep forest climbing spectacular native sacred ground up to the cliff dwellings.

Beneath contaminated soil are the graves of tribes long since reduced or destroyed by a manifest destiny that had broken every promise and now having split the atom can't heal it back together again.

And then I realized that the Alamo comes from that same derivation, and must once have been called *los alamos* as well. But by the time they were fighting to make it part of America only one tree was left standing.

During World War II, Wavy Gravy, then Hugh Romney, yet to be Merry Prankster and Woodstock healer, lived two blocks away from me. We attended P.S. #16 together. When we met, he was in third grade and I in second.

On the street between Wavy's and mine lived a new fellow in the neighborhood with whom I became friendly. In days when separated families were a rarity, he lived in a most unique situation. He had a four-bedroom house to himself with only a housekeeper to account to. He did not want to speak about his mother, said she was perhaps dead, and when I asked about his father, he stiffened and fell silent.

One day, when we were playing in his basement rec room, I mentioned something about my father and he stopped cold, looked down, then angrily shook his head, and bid me follow him. Upstairs, behind a thick door, was a room with only a single bed and a dresser in it. It was bare as any convent cell, except on the wall above the bed where a crucifix might be hung there was a German machine-pistol.

He hurried us back out of the room. "Don't tell anyone, but my father is in the army and it's a big, big secret!"

"Where is he?" I asked.

"Not sure," he said, "but it's something to do with Manhattan and I never ever see him."

My friend, who I am told violently imploded as a teenager, was one of the first casualties of atomic warfare. His father was one of the generals in charge of the Manhattan Project. He was away for years "making the bomb" in Los Alamos.

At P.S. #16 they told Gravy, the general's son, and me we were going to die.

Duck and cover! Leave a neat pile of ash.

Some years ago a fellow approached us during a break in an afternoon workshop and asked if we would visit his wife, in a coma in the Los Alamos hospital just a few minutes away.

Ondrea's work with people in coma is widely known. The meeting with his comatose wife, and the messages transmitted, were very productive. This led him to gather a group of fellow scientists from the lab for something of a spirit-meets-science meditation group. But it didn't work. Their lack of trust in anything they could not touch or control (physically or mentally) caused them, as our son Noah might say, "to meditate with one eye open."

They were pridefully rational and seemed almost amoral, regarding discussions of topics such as the importance of compassion versus efficiency as mental weakness. But they weren't heartless, just suffering the fallout of living in a realm where such considerations were not encouraged by their employer.

If it were not for the forced opening of the collective mind to the possibility of complete annihilation, would we be prepared for the absolute necessity for forgiveness and compassion that may keep the world from destroying itself?

Can we use the bomb like death over our left shoulder to more fully appreciate life? The bomb represents our failed aspirations, our dissatisfaction, our doubt, distrust, and fear. We have become so world-weary, we kill our children without noticing them lying in the streets, in doorways, and on heating grates.

Some part of us has, like Machiavelli, chosen fear over love.

The New World has grown ill with neglect. Frogs have six legs. Fish and friends covered with carposi.

And they say in a couple of generations the songbirds may be gone.

There's not a moment to lose.

Consider kindness with your last breath.

TWENTY-EIGHT

mother's day

The first name of creation is Mother of Us All. As we genuflect at the altar behind the brow, praying to be free from our image of perfection to which so much suffering clings, she puts her arms around us and bids us lay our head on her shoulder, whispering, "Don't you know that with all your fear and anger all you are fit for is love?"

Stepping out onto the front deck last October, looking across our little valley, Ondrea and I recalled that time twenty years before at the Columbia Presbyterian Children's Hospital when, sitting beside a dying child's bed as she passed from her body, I felt her being lifted away by what appeared to be Mother Mary. And all too sad and rational, I had asked at that inner altar, when 250,000 people die every day, how was it possible for the Mother of Compassion to be there for all of them? How could she bundle all the dying children to her heart? And the mystery replied, "When a thousand people look at the moon, there are a thousand moons!"

Breaking our reverie, we looked up into the brilliant high-mountain sky quite amazed and saw suspended about two hundred feet above us *a huge silver exclamation mark* on whose side was written "VIRGIN" in large bright blue letters.

We laughed and called out to the Mother or the inhabitants of the basket below the hot-air balloon, whichever answered first.

Dropping a hundred feet or so, they called out to ask if they might land, as their adventure had gone amiss. They had left Albuquerque, more than a hundred miles to the south, as part of the Balloon Festival the day before, but troubling air currents had kept them from rising over the Sangre de Cristo Mountains to our southeast and "the race was over."

They came down in the sage mesa at the rim of the valley. We hooked a rope to our car and pulled them, still ten feet off the ground, to an open area where their balloon would not be ripped by sage or cactus on the mesa. Here their chase crew could find a road that gave them access to the deconstruction of the sizable apparatus. It was one of the balloons owned by Richard Branson, of Virgin Atlantic Airlines, and piloted by Par Lindstrom, who some months later with two others attempted once again to circumnavigate the planet in a hot-air balloon.

But this balloon, Par explained, was not lifted by hot air but by helium, a less often used buoyant. And the balloon needed to be deflated so the chase crew, when they eventually caught up with them, could fold it and pack it onto the truck.

Two approximately ten-foot flaps were opened at top of the balloon as it lay on its side and Par and his navigator pushed down on the narrow end of the huge sack and worked the helium up toward Ondrea and me as we held open the large flaps with outstretched arms.

The rush of high-atmosphere-cooled helium, $2,200 worth, Par sighed, enveloped us. There was only this helium wind absorbing us, our voices climbing back to where the helium had cooled . . . and laughing and laughing higher.

Then too many heliums, no oxygen, anoxia, very heavy heartbeat, remember the ground beneath your feet . . . too dry to laugh . . . helium and human molecules mixing. Leaning out of the helium river to get a fresh breath.

The balloon flattened, and us too beneath a ponderosa. The chase crew arrived, the blue letters disappearing into expert folds. Dust settling from their departure.

And back to the altar to see what next She of the Mystery has in Mind.

She speaks only of love and service. Reminding us that Neem Karoli once said if he hadn't been so compassionate, he could have been a great saint. She bids us forgo sainthood for the benefit of all sentient beings.

TWENTY-NINE

a devotional leaning

Once I asked the Dalai Lama if he ever experienced fear. He said he felt not only fear at times, but anxiety. When I asked him what he did when such confusion arose, he said he went for counsel to his advisors. One of which, he added, was 850 years old.

We converse with a sense of oneness, at the edge of duality, with the mystery personified in the heart as our deep-wisdom teachers. My advisor on that level has long been Maharaji, Neem Karoli Baba, who I initially encountered through Ram Dass's *Be Here Now*. Maharaji "threw his blanket over me" (took me under his wing) almost the first time I spoke his name. He did the same for an astonished Ondrea seven years later.

Maharaji was closely linked with Hanuman, a remarkable transcendent animal spirit. One of the most remarkable personifications of devotion and selfless service in the classic Hindu holy book the *Ramayana*.

In the *Ramayana* Hanuman served Ram, a manifestation of God, without reserve. Indeed, he nearly defines devotional practice (bhakti yoga), and to show how complete his absorption in the sacred, he pulls open his chest to reveal the name of God written on every bone in his body. RAM RAM RAM RAM RAM RAM.

Hanuman holding open his chest to display the heart of devotion is one of the most popular sacred images in India. This bloody tearing open to reveal our true nature may be reminiscent of the image of Jesus hanging from the cross. Though their images seem quite different— one teaches us how to live, the other how to die—their blood is the same.

As Gandhi spoke his name for God—RAM, RAM, RAM—three times as he fell shot through the heart, Hanuman and Jesus were One.

The more we know of Maharaji, the less any physical form fits. He took on form as fat old grandpa or brilliant teacher as was needed. He was a third-eye chart. The further you could see, the less he was out there and the more he was felt within.

The more we see him not as just an old body farting and filled with love, the less we see ourselves as anything other than that love. Until he was just the wind, a thought, a moment of bliss. A reason to live and a reason not to fear death.

I have often felt he appears as he does in his photos out of compassion for the emulsion on our only photographic memory. As deft as Hanuman at serving the sacred, Maharaji, some even say, was his incarnation. It is said Hanuman, a great spirit warrior, defeater of the demon Ravana and the ten thousand hindrances, acts, as he did between Sita and Ram, as a messenger between the devotee and the object of devotion. His message is, "You are part of the mind of God."

When students asked Neem Karoli Baba how to raise their *kundalini* (essential spirit power, primal energy connection), expecting complex instruction, he simply said, "Just love everybody."

Sometimes I weep when I hear his name.

Meeting the truth like Maharaji at level after level, one comes to realize that true devotion does not stop at any form, no matter how beautiful or sacred.

Only edgeless presence continues. Nothing to obstruct lucidity or distract us from the ground of being.

Hanuman knew it well when he said to Ram, "When I do not know who I am I serve You. But when I know who I am I am You."

The closer we get, the less we experience That as a person, but rather all together beyond personage. Not the creator, but creation. Boundary-less essence, indefinable but directly experiencable as the clarity of love.

Devotional contemplation draws the mind into the heart and keeps it directed toward the sacred. Mindfulness or insight meditation, culti-vating a merciful awareness, draws the heart into mind, and observes the sacred everywhere it looks.

These seemingly separate practices join at many levels. They have a considerable willingness to explore beyond their edge in common, without which real progress cannot be made. Each practice attempts to overcome forgetfulness and rejoices in remembering. And though one school of thought may speak of self and the other of no-self, they are both referring to the same essence. Though each may display different bumper stickers, each wishes only to be free and reside in the truth. And the Great Desire, the will toward mystery, is the central motiva-tion to their lives.

What remains when we have gone beyond everything? As the Thai Master said, "The truth remains!" The indestructible truth.

Maharaji, when I call to you in the middle of the night, you show me what keeps us separate. How far from selfless is my love, how much wanting there still is within my giving. How readily the mind bends toward old pain.

I can only surrender. Letting go of even my suffering.

The choir applauds as the music begins and, looking like my old rabbi, you remind me to listen to my cells and love with all my being and with all my heart. And to keep the mystery as for frontlets between my eyes.

Then you arise in the heart once again and I can sleep.

THIRTY

his holiness
the dalai lama

Everyone who has met His Holiness the Dalai Lama, one of the great persons of our time, perhaps a living Buddha, has some wonderful story to tell. Here is mine.

When I was one of six people on a panel with His Holiness for three days in southern California in fall, 1989 (the week he was awarded the Nobel prize), we had much wonderful dialogue about the dharma and particularly the work we were presently doing with those in great grief.

On the third day, while we were in an investigative discussion about the protection of those in need and particularly the nature of anger, he said that there was no room for anger: "Cut off all anger." And asked me, "What do you think about this?"

I was so engaged by his dialogue with the other panelists I really didn't know quite what to say. But I replied that I thought we were trying to find another way to deal with anger beside suppressing it. And I heard myself say, with a *chutzpah* bordering on brain damage, to the

Dharma King of the Middle Way, that we were searching for a new paradigm, "*a middle way* between the expression of anger and noninjury" in which anger could still arise in the mind, but we were learning to mindfully respond instead of compulsively react to it.

And he asked, "But if it comes into the mind, won't it also come out the mouth?"

To which I replied, "If it comes into the mind wholeheartedly there is no compulsion to act on it. It can float in space."

And though he smiled supportively, I heard in my heart, as I had heard him say before, that anger was too dangerous to fool around with! "Rid yourself of it for the benefit of all sentient beings. It is better to express the pain before it turns to suffering and erupts as hostility. To bring forth world peace there must be mental peace."

When I asked if we needed to be wholly without attachment in order to be free, he said, "No attachment, no compassion!" To be truly compassionate we must be equal with all life, superior to nothing or no one.

When asked what his favorite visualization was, the Dalai Lama said that, though it might sound odd to our Western ear, it was that of a wounded animal lying very still meditating for days in an isolated place.

That evening at a closing celebration for the participants, there were perhaps three hundred people standing about in a large open room awaiting the promised blessing ceremony by the Dalai Lama.

By the time Ondrea and I arrived, still perhaps forty-five minutes before he was to join the group, there was already a long line forming to receive a *kata,* a blessing scarf of soft gauzelike cotton placed about the neck by His Holiness. The room was abuzz with warm discussions. At the head of the line was an old friend with whom I was speaking when the Dalai Lama arrived. As I stepped back to go to the end of the line, His Holiness reached out a hand and drew me toward him. I told him I wasn't really in line, but he shook his head and pulled me closer. Holding my hand, he turned toward one of his monks and queried where the *katas* were.

There seemed some confusion among the monks. The *katas* were not ready. With his free left hand he pointed and scolded the monks for not being prepared. There was fire coming out of his left hand, while from his right hand tenderly holding mine I felt nothing but love. He was at that moment the living truth of what I had previously suggested as a middle way between heaven and hell. And it was clear that it might take a Buddha to pull it off successfully. That it was easier to speak of "dharmic anger for the benefit of others" than it was to remain whole while attempting such a dangerously self-manifesting dualistic state.

But the teaching was far from over. Standing in the midst of the crowd a bit prideful perhaps for being personally pulled aside by the Dalai Lama, I was approached by his doctor, who came over to me and said, "The Dalai Lama said he is one scarf short and needs to take your *kata* back. It will be returned by the end of the evening." And so the *kata* upon which much attachment had been bestowed disappeared back into his remarkable hands.

And I, who had perhaps thought himself for a moment too "special" to have to wait in line, had to wait for hours. Until frustration and attachment had been well replaced by warmth and patience. The room had half emptied before the scarf was returned, twice blessed.

And I was thrice blessed to process it all with Ondrea, to uncover the next level of holding that was capable of obstructing clarity.

But the teaching from one such as the Dalai Lama never ends if one is paying attention.

About ten years later, in 1998, another opportunity arose. In San Francisco for the World Peace Conference, the Dalai Lama and I met with the other teachers who would be on a panel with us. I doubted he remembered our meeting ten years before until one of the committee reminded him of our previous interchange. He smiled broadly, and once again took my hand and asked what I had been up to lately. He kept shaking his head yes when I told him that my most recent book, *A Year to Live*, was inspired by *his* comment a few years before, when asked, at fifty-eight years old, what he intended to do with the rest of his life and he replied, "Prepare for death."

As the small group disbanded, I found myself the last to leave as the Dalai Lama reached out and put his arm around my waist. And I put my arm about his. As we came side by side to the door, I thought I must not inconvenience him in any way and began to loosen my arm about his waist, but he did not loosen his and we walked somehow simultaneously through that doorway.

As we approached the two long double flights of steel stairs that descended to the auditorium, neither of us changed our contact in the least. Though there was noticeable consternation on the part of his bodyguards and attendants that, descending arm in arm, he might, if I was the least out of step, fall and be injured.

The two flights were traversed as though on an escalator. Only if I thought was it dangerous.

And the next day I received an apple from the teacher.

At a bookstore in Marin County for a short talk and a book signing, about to be introduced by my old teacher and ever receptive spiritual friend Jack Kornfield, I am handed an apple conveyed from the Dalai Lama.

An apple from the teacher of my teachers, which Ondrea and I naturally passed on as the next teaching to the audience. Everyone was offered a bite whether they came up with a book to be signed or not.

The first bites were taken as of the Eucharist, mantras humming in the cortex, blessings, blessings everywhere. But soon the apple took on a handled look, all the "clean" bite places had been consumed. Only others' teeth marks and fingerprints remained. The fearless nibbling continued. And the apple continued to slowly brown and seemingly wither. Only the most heroic, the recently vaccinated, and Christian Scientists could brave the mental barrier of microbes and a certain Ganges attraction/repulsion to manage a nip from the fading flesh.

And the room had a certain joy.

THIRTY-ONE

to walk and sleep,
to dream and eat
in the mystery

As we become human beings we inhabit a new body, the body of awareness. Sleeping, dreaming, and eating take on new meaning and opportunity.

We learn anew to breath and even walk. When walking mindfully, as we slow down and attend to all the intentions and sensations that go into making a single step, we realize we hardly even know how to walk.

As in all rebirths into deeper levels of ourselves, we must, in a manner of speaking, be born again, learning to talk and walk, even to eat and sleep, in a new gravity. On new terrain, with new legs, inspired to go forward by the fear that signals you are approaching your edge, beyond which all growth occurs, and the delight of the eternally new.

Clarity follows mindfulness. Completion follows forgiveness. Compassion follows empathy. Wisdom rests in being. Miracles abound!

The miracle alchemizes the ordinary. Eating, sleeping, dreaming become at times miraculous.

There is a Zen story about two students of well-known teachers meeting while drawing water. One inquires about the other's teacher's accomplishments. To which, with a wide swing of his arm, the student tells of his teacher's ability to fly and foretell the future.

"Ah," said the other, "very impressive. But my teacher's abilities are greater yet. When she walks she only walks. When she eats she only eats. Even when she sleeps she remains present. And when she dreams she only dreams. She is simply present."

It is a teaching tale that reminds one, with that half-smile the Buddha recommended, to remain mindful in each physical and mental posture.

To simply walk while walking, and talk when talking. Not off elsewhere in thought, but present in one's actions. Present in the present.

TO EAT, SLEEP, DREAM IN THE MYSTERY

For some months during a period of intense practice, I, like innumerable yogis and edge-players before me and during me, attempted to stay awake in my sleep. Not only aware of, and often in, my dreams, but mindful of the body as well.

I slept in what is called the corpse, or mummy, position: on my back with my arms at my sides. Attempting to maintain that posture throughout the night.

If an arm repositioned itself or my head bent into the pillow, it was immediately returned to its original position.

After a few dozen nights the body no longer moved in its sleep. When someone said that watching me sleep was like a visit to the morgue, I knew the process was well under way.

Of course this kind of focus on the field of sensation allows one to be almost immediately aware of changes in the dream or body state.

One is present at the inception of the dream or the sensation (or even the intention to move that precedes the movement), participating in the unfolding.

A few months into this process, I awoke one night in the corpse position and as usual swung my attention directly to the breath. But it did not land on the breath, or even the thought of the breath. It seemed somehow to slip past all that.

And suddenly the corner of the mind peeled back. I could see beyond the goings-on moving across the screen.

I could see behind the images on the screen a vast universe that included an almost cartoonlike image of myself peeking behind the screen of consciousness.

That glimpse "backstage" was another reinforcement of the repeated assurance that we are not the mind. Nor are we the images thereon. Not even the thought that thinks itself. Mind is an artifact, a fading photograph of the last instant, the vanishing footsteps of the wandering soul.

The closest I could get to describing how it felt to watch the mind from outside the mind ("Well, then, who's watching?!" says the rational suffering; and, indeed, that's always the question) is to say that I was just an innocent bystander. Just the space it was all happening in. Just the witness-awareness that, brushing over reality, brings ghostly objects to life as consciousness, as thought, as something to cast shadows. Not the ordinary mind in which floats all we mistake for our final frontier, but the space between and behind.

Behind it all we are the light by which we see.

Before the word you were.

Part of the wakeful sleeping exercise is the mindful awakening practice.

Recognizing the first sensations upon awakening, you focus on the feeling of that first breath in whose midst you find yourself. Noticing whether it is the in-breath or out-breath into which you awoke just before awakening. Neither is preferable; it's just a focusing exercise. Staying with that mindfulness of breath for a minute or two before proceeding with your life.

PERCHANCE TO DREAM

There is more to sleep than we dream. But not more than we *can* dream.

We fall asleep and show up for work. Drifting off, we slide out of this body and into a luminous lab coat to continue our research in the laboratory.

Sleep is an experiment in wakefulness. It is the trance that can break the trance.

When experimenting with hypnosis in high school and for a few years thereafter, I would on occasion put fully induced subjects under their own control. I would tell them they would do whatever they told themselves to do, to open their eyes and take it from there. Still of course with the proviso that I could break the induction with a few chosen words. Often it seemed that, within a few minutes of wandering about the room and open-eyed communication, their trance was no longer in effect. But if I said to them even a half-hour later that I was going to bring them out of it, they would show considerable consternation and often plead to be allowed to remain in that totally wakeful, completely dreaming state.

When we know we are dreaming, we are awake. When we wake from the dream and know that wakefulness is also a dream, we become "awakened."

The masterful Taoist poet-philosopher Chang Tzu queries, "Am I a man dreaming I am a butterfly or a butterfly dreaming I am a man?" *Both of course*, depending on whether it is the dream-body or gravity-body we are wearing at the time.

In dream, as in waking, the observed is the observer.

We dream ourselves in a thousand forms, wondering how long it might take to recognize ourselves. And to love ourselves when we are no longer recognizable.

We say we are thinking about dream, but in truth we are dreaming about thought. Thought and dream are the same. Images float up from that same nowhere, dissolving one into the next. Images materialize from thin air. They seem to just think themselves, and disappear like rain into a river.

Thought and dream follow the same process, even the same logic, gravity or not.

Though they follow the same path, dream is more reliable. It takes life full-heartedly. In thought there is the tendency to filter out the "inconsequential and distracting," the other three-quarters of the available reality. The intercession of interpretation alters the raw bio-electrical input of the senses as they make contact with the wary instincts that receive them. Our world is neutered by interpretation.

The angels have told me another secret in my dreams, which I can't remember upon waking. Only a sense of being taught, of learning, and an odd delight remain.

We awake some mornings as if returning from a monastery, new insights fresh in our mind, our hearts more spacious. Our body too, as yet unaccustomed to gravity, feeling quite distinctly as though it is falling upward. Grabbing the blankets to keep from falling toward the ceiling.

All pretty strange! All oddly gratifying and reassuring.

A feeling of boundless space predominating. A buoyancy in which float thought and feeling and sensation as they act themselves out. Thoughts think themselves, feel themselves, taste themselves. Sensations experience.

Somehow I know something more than I knew yesterday. I do not know exactly what that is, but the universe seems to be floating in something greater. The space between atoms, the space between planets, "all same." Levels of being momentarily revealed. A truth that cannot be "known," but only experienced.

It is as though I have read some great book in my sleep whose contents I cannot recall, but whose effects persevere even after the words have disappeared.

Upon leaving such dream teachings, the lessons seem to recede into the heart, welcoming us to the path that awakens.

SOMETIMES DREAMS MEASURE OUR HEALING

A dreamlike vision reflecting the work of uncovering and forgiveness actually occurred during a meditation retreat. I noticed the smell of something burning. Looking about me, I saw the huddled masses thrown from the boxcars. The smell of urine and wet wool. Children crying, men and women sobbing, and the bark of ferocious dogs. And the acrid smell of smoke rising from the crematorium chimneys.

Before us stood a scrubbed S.S. officer with shiny boots and a riding crop in his hand slapping each in the face to drive them to the right or to the left.

Tears pouring from beneath closed eyelids, I remember feeling a sort of pride at how compassionate I was, how identified with the victim, how pure.

And the bell rang and I rose from my *zafu* feeling I was doing quite well with my compassion practice, and how rid of the angry child I seemed to be.

After thirty minutes of walking meditation, greedy for the next "compassion experience," I moved quickly back to my meditation cushion. Like one who has risen in the middle of a dream and attempts to return rapidly to continue the dream, I settled back into the meditation. Within perhaps fifteen minutes I detected the acrid smell again.

Oh, what a sympathetic being I was to be able to access so readily the heart of the suffering! And I again opened my dream eyes to look about at my fellow prisoners and saw instead, as from a worm's-eye view, first shiny leather boots and then, panning upward, the swastika on my belt buckle. And I broke into a cold sweat.

In my manicured hand a riding crop, striking women and children and men to the right, to the gas chambers, and to the left, to work or founder in illness until they dropped. He was the worst part of us all, perfect for the job.

He was what Elisabeth Kübler-Ross used to call "our Hitler." I believe I experienced more healing from the second vision than even the first. It excluded nothing from the heart work to be done.

Which recalls another dream. The one a year later that displayed so lightly the healing that was sinking from the mind into the heart. I dreamed I was as usual after a workshop meeting with a line of attendees who had some questions. And up came Adolf Hitler himself, head bowed, a bit embarrassed that others might overhear his difficulty-in-relationship question. Not getting along so well with Eva and what could he do to make their relationship work. And seeing how downhearted he seemed, I put my arm around his shoulders, and we walked off a bit from the crowd so that he might feel a little more at ease in talking about his feelings. I felt for him what I might for anyone. He was my brother in pain.

And I bow ten thousand times to the healing revealed in dreams projected on the surface of our heart.

In dreams we follow each adventure. There are no distractions. Just love and fear. Just the dream as it is.

Some say it is easier to become conscious in our dreams, perhaps because we wholeheartedly accept their logic, than it is to be mindful when we consider ourselves awake. Because in dreams we are not imprisoned by the distorted perceptions/interpretations of the "rational" mind.

But of course if you've been paying attention, you have noticed there is no rational mind. There is in its place only a fright-filled concept. More a mirror than a window for the instability we sequester in our infinitely insecure relationship to the *underdream*, from which who we think we are, and who we fear we are, arises.

Last night I dreamed we could enter now the source directly. That the grace we are was wholly unobstructed.

It reminded me of another dream years ago when I stepped from the boat wondering how to be lighter than water, and walked on the sea. Water walking on water, just a couple of sacred molecules dancing with each other.

One teacher used to ask me what my face was before I was born. He wanted to know who I was before that first thought, before I started dreaming.

THIRTY-TWO

eating karma

When a continuity of mindfulness is sustained during long periods of practice, it is not uncommon to find oneself quite naturally eating, as well as walking and dreaming, in a conscious manner. Directly participating in the process from moment to moment.

Sitting down to lunch after a particularly quiet morning, I noticed as I raised that first spoon to my lips that something was very different.

What followed did not so much offer insight into eating as it did a clearer seeing of something much deeper. Something closer to our deepest hunger for understanding and freedom.

As I began to eat, as I lifted the spoon to my mouth, it stopped in midair. I had to remind it to continue for the spoon to reach my lips. I had to continually reestablish the intention that precedes every action for it to maintain its momentum.

Each moment was wholly discrete. Each mind moment was separate and distinct, not at all part of an automatic forward tumbling of one thought into another as in the ordinary habituation of consciousness. Each moment being wholly new depended on a wholly renewed motivation to hold its course.

The karma, the momentum, that kept the spoon heading toward my mouth constantly dissolving and having to be reestablished once again.

The teachings about intention being the basis of karma, that what and how we want defines what and how we get, clear as the spoon suspended motionless in midair. What moved the spoon, like what propels our life, is intention.

The next spoon raised after an eternity of chewing was like stop-motion photography, or as though seen in the discrete flashings of a strobe light.

It was a bit like Salvador Dalí's melting watches. Time kept stopping if I didn't keep it going. The spoon would have hung in midair. It seemed like it took a very long time to get from the plate to my tongue. Like hauling freight between galaxies.

The more I ate, the more there seemed to be on the plate. Was I going to spend infinity in a bowl of stir-fry?!

Each millisecond had a clearly enunciated beginning, middle, and end. (It was not a kind of slow motion, but rather an accelerated observation of subtle detail in the process of thought. A magnification of the elements.)

Lifting the spoon . . . no past, no present . . . just luminous presence.

The spoon in the grasp of the process, karmaless, submerged in the inseparable flow of Tao.

Watching the intention that preceded each action. Noting the intention to stand before standing, to lift the arm, to scratch. Clearly the motivation that arises from wanting and the urge it produces moved the spoon all by itself.

Recognizing that unconscious momentum could be disengaged from desire by not automatically following its intention, the mind filled with the delight of possible liberation. *Karma interruptus.* By noting intention from its inception and staying mindful of its inner changes, its natural impermanence will carry it away and compulsive activity could be stayed in midair.

A similar phenomenon sometimes occurs during the walking meditation. In the walking practice one maintains mindfulness of the sensations that accompany each aspect of each step. Noting "lifting" as the foot rises off the ground, "placing" as the foot swings forward, and "putting" as the foot touches the floor. Along with noting the changing flow of sensation that accompanies each step, and the motion thereof, intention is also closely noted.

One usually uses about fifteen feet or so for the walking practice before mindfully stopping and turning for the return trip across the continent. Noting the intention to stop. Turning very slowly with close attention to each movement in that turn. Noting the slight angling of one foot after the other intending to turn.

One day, noting the multiple intentions it took for even a simple turn, one foot moving about 45 degrees from the last, ever so slowly turning. At the end of the 180-degree turn, the intention to stop just floated like a bubble through the "watching only." But no identification with the intention to stop arose with it. Just a pleasant watching of its habitual recurrence a few more times until it fell silent. And to my amazement the body just kept turning all by itself. Slowly turning in a full circle and continuing to turn, fascinated by the bewildering ride.

Comprehending the dependent origination of desire's effect on intention, and intention's effect on action, we demagnetize karma. All that sleepwalking, all those meals eaten but never tasted or appreciated, discontinued from creating more of the same.

Offered to the mystery, to the heart that knows the longing, as the Native Americans say, to walk, even to eat, in a sacred manner.

FOOD TEACHES US HOW TO PRAY

When I was very young, my mother made a reticent child pray each night:

Thank you for this life so sweet.
Thank you for the food we eat.
Thank you for the birds that sing.
Thank you God for everything!

It meant nothing at the time. Now meditating before sleep to recall with gratitude the day seems less frivolous all the time.

Even in my most devotional periods I was never much for prayer. Although I was introduced to prayer as something of a bedtime ritual, it never engaged my heart.

But as the depth of mind we call heart became more distinct, I began to pray before eating.

What began as an experiment in consciousness, *a remembering* in the form of a bit of reverential prayer theater, led to a wholly unexpected deepening in my practice.

Evolving from the numb repetitions of youth and the guises and gestures of spiritual adolescence, the prayer, at first mostly external, began to penetrate through the stratum of mind until it entered the heart.

For decades I usually turned to the mystery before I ate. The prayers changing to reflect the maturations of the heart.

At first I just generally thanked the universe.

Then years later I thanked the food as a child of the earth, visualizing the wheat in the field, the water in the stream, the soybean or the cow in green pasture.

Then later yet the prayer became action. It became a mindful exploration of what exactly all this eating was all about. Not thinking the meal but present in my body at the table. The field of sensation under close scrutiny. Mindful of the cold of the utensil in my hand, mindful of it gradually warming to my touch. Mindful of the muscles extending and contracting with each forkful raised to the opened maw of the mouth. Mindful of the touch of food on the tongue. Attentive to the utensil returning to the plate for more. Watching the gradual unfolding of tastes evolving on the tongue. The intention, the desire, before each mouthful noticed. Chewing a moment at a time before the food is pushed down the gullet. The fork lined up like a dump truck at a construction site, waiting to haul away its next load.

Exploring any drive as powerful as hunger, much less the longing for particular tastes, with mercy and awareness benefits the eater as well as the eaten.

Eating consciously, mindfully, slows the passing blur. Like looking at a snapshot of a runner in full extension and wondering how one can maintain balance with both feet off the ground. And we put our fork back down on the table. Chewing taste to taste, not suspending the spoon like a steamshovel in front of the mouth waiting for us to swallow so it can dump its next load. Not waiting for the next taste even while chewing. Feeling the tongue move the food in the mouth, noting how its consistency is changing. Acknowledging too the intention to swallow. Noting the sound of the shovel scraping the plate as it scoops up another batch.

So many times around a large table a group of people holding hands in prayer before eating, each opening our eyes nearly in love well sated before the first conscious mouthful.

The silence before eating less a prayer and more a communion with the sacred.

Then through a kind of joyous attachment I began in silence offering my meals to our late beloved teacher, Neem Karoli Baba, Maharaji.

Though at first it seemed a bit too much in form for this Buddhist-conditioned boy, it soon became quite something else. A means of maintaining a surprisingly open conduit to Maharaji's energy and voice in my heart.

What began as a somewhat playful and rather picturesque offering up of the contents of my plate to Maharaji *became a transfer of hearts*.

One day he stopped me in mid-thank and said, "Stop with offering me the meals! Stop with the prayers! Only love will do!!

"Before you eat, take a few breaths into your heart and wait until love becomes your state of being. Don't offer me anything but love."

This communing with Maharaji that passed for prayer became a simple breathing into the heart. Sensations gradually intensified in my chest until the heart felt like an open conduit through which was rushing a universe of energy. It was an opening as great as any that loving-kindness meditation had so far revealed.

Now I must love before I eat. Whoever would have imagined that the act of taking so clearly represented in our eating could be converted to a sense of giving? Blessing the food. Reflecting with gratitude on our friends and teachers. Sitting mindfully, heartfully, in our bodies appreciating the process we are eating: the process we have been. *Bon appétit!*

Food taught me to pray while my teacher taught me to breathe, and all before the food or the heart got cold.

Eventually we come to eat in a sacred manner. Honoring the eater and the eaten by entering the eating with mercy and awareness, conscious of their interconnected, even interdependent, nature.

We approach the table reflecting on the death-defying act of eating. Exploring from bite to bite, from moment to moment, the field of sensation as well as the ever changing nature of desire. We feel ourselves a part of the process of life and death. We are the eater who will eventually be eaten. We are in harmony with the perfect pendulum of nature (some call it Shiva's Mahalila, the Great Dance of Nature).

When we live in a sacred manner, we eat life now, not as a questionable aftertaste on the deathbed.

There is another way in which eating has taught Ondrea and me how to pray. It has made reliquaries of a few early '80s Chinese restaurants in San Francisco, around whose largest circular tables we sat with so many AIDS patients after workshops. The sacred relic their long-recalled bright talk and good-hearted laughter. All those God-loving, chow-mein-stuffed bodies now turned to soil, turned to flowers and shiny red worms that praise the mystery with every turn.

THIRTY-THREE

the animal spirits

I have for most of my life received remarkable teachings on how to be a human being from the animal spirits.

It was their invitation that began my opening and it is still that quality of wholeness experienced on the land that regulates the beat of my heart.

When I first heard someone say that in fifty years all the songbirds might be extinct, it worried that song learned so long ago from the thrushes. Waking as a child, listening silent in my warm morning bed.

It broke the heart that recalled that robin shot with my BB gun. The pride of accuracy instantly vanishing when I saw the torn bird empty on the grass.

If there are no birds, who will transmit from the ledge outside the frightened child's window that somehow everything is going to be okay: that we are an integral part of something very big and indescribably beautiful.

THE ANIMAL TEACHINGS

Fire Sermon of the Ants

Attempting to rouse his monks to yet greater commitment to practice, the Buddha gave what has come to be known as the Fire Sermon, in which he said something to the effect that the eyes are on fire, the tongue is on fire, the ears are on fire, the mind is on fire. And suggested we quench it with the cool stillness of the dharma.

Some years ago dharma benefactor Margaret Austin, in the process of converting a portion of her ranch outside Houston into a meditation facility for the community, invited Ondrea and me to lead a weekend retreat.

A two-day meditation retreat conducted in complete silence and committed to fifteen to eighteen hours a day of sitting and walking practice can give one's daily practice quite a boost in concentration and a considerable resurgence of energy.

On the second day, the group well settled into the regimen, the group concentration beginning to envelope us, we were on a mid-afternoon group mindfulness walk. Following an old cow path through an open field, I led a few dozen retreatants on a meditation in which we each watched the feet of the person ahead of us and lifted our feet as they lifted theirs, and so on, while being thoroughly submerged in the sensations that accompanied each step.

When the practice is done in a circle, you soon realize that as the person before you is setting your pace, so you are setting the pace of the one behind you. In fact, you come to realize you are ultimately just following yourself.

Leading the group slowly, halfway across the pasture I noticed in my closely observed field of sensation a burning in my right calf as though struck by a metallic spark. Duly noting the new sensation, I continued with another step before the multiple fiery insinuations into the open calm of the walking meditation caused me to less than mindfully look down to find that I was leading the group through a large nest of fire ants.

Most were bravely attempting to "just be mindful" of the stinging assault, while busy doing something like the Irish stomp to shake loose some of the ants now well above their knees. Soon the group looked, as they jumped about raising the red Texas dust, backlit by a huge crimson sun, like red shamans dancing their hearts out to rid this world of confusion. Stomping and laughing and yelping bodhisattvas come to wake the earth, to split it open, to beckon the Ocean of Compassion. Drawn kicking and hooting into the fiery center of each bite, into the molten center of the earth, into the heart freed of fear and distrust. Dancing for our enlightenment, to free and save us all from that which, rising up, makes us weak in the knees.

The Half-a-Cat Teachings

Somewhere along the way I was entrusted with a half-paralyzed cat.

I used to bring her with me to the Unity Press office in a shoebox. Off to one side on my desk she could be turned and fed as need be. It may have been Joseph Goldstein, while working on his book, who first called her "Shoebox."

The paralysis, the veterinarian said, made her "half a cat, a brain-oriented genetic failure" the effects of whose disease would progress up the body from unusable back legs to the inability to move and eventually to breathe. He reached out as if to take "this problem" off our hands. We replaced young Shoebox in her palanquin and off we went.

Three weeks and a hundred doses of a slowly swallowed concoction of warm olive oil with a smidge of garlic and long massages later, the paralysis halted just before it overtook her front legs. Gradually it began to reverse itself. Six weeks later the sick cat brought to me for some sort of animal last rites was doing the two-step on my meditation pillow.

But there was a moment before she was well, when, on her come-back, on what appeared to be a very bad day for her, she seemed to be losing strength very rapidly as the paralysis advanced back up her body. Meditating near her, I heard her drag her back legs as she pulled toward me. So I lay with my back flat on the floor and put her on my chest thinking she might just die there. And let her just ride on the slow breath of meditation. About ten minutes into this process, she made a rasping breath and, it seemed, stopped breathing.

And I, half in faith and half immersed in some episode of mystery theater, the real illusion of birth and death, breathed my "breath energy" heart to heart back into her limp body. Perhaps she had not died or she had a little kitty NDE (near-death experience) and discovered her body, like ours, was rented not owned, but with a shudder she began once again to breathe. As she opened her eyes close to mine, I think I smelled a little garlic when she burped.

Some months later, at 3:00 A.M. she jumped onto my bed, turned her rear end to the side of my face, and pushed her first baby into my ear.

The Weeping-Bull Teachings

One Sunday afternoon in my 1964 drug bardo (a bardo is, in the *Tibetan Book of the Dead*, sometimes designated as an interstice between lives), misled by the braggadocio of old ghosts, I attended the bull ring just outside Mexico City.

There was nothing heroic there. In fact, after two "brave bulls" had been ceremoniously slaughtered, the torero doors swung open and the third sacrifice entered the ring.

It did not charge out snorting and bucking, as had the others. It was shoved reluctantly into the ring. It did not want to fight. It ran from the matador. It bellowed and pled. It was not a death-black, square-shouldered fighting bull, but a brown steer that looked like someone had sold a pet 4-H project to the wrong vaquero. The "bull" was terrified and ran around and around the ring. When the picadors pierced its hide, it shrieked for help. The matador was young and flustered and missed several passes, only further wounding and terrifying the animal, which ran about looking for escape.

After many failed passes by the clearly disturbed matador, the crowd, horrified by this blatantly unheroic scene, went mad with mercy and rage. It began to stomp and yell, *"Mata lo, mata lo,"* "Kill it, kill it," again and again as the poor animal wailed in terror. *Mata lo! Mata lo! Mata lo!* A compassionate rage vibrating the blood-spattered walls of the torero.

At last with an awful bellow from the steer and an anguished wail from the audience, the bull was killed dead as Lorca at the firing wall.

We experienced compassion and rage in the same moment. The crowd was on its feet shouting at the inexperienced matador. There was even a sense of danger to the matador, a feeling that at any moment someone might spontaneously jump into the bull ring as *novicieros* occasionally do to prove their courage, but this time to dispatch the matador and save the bull. People were stamping their feet in outrage, "Kill it, kill it, have mercy kill it!"

Not the least of the lessons from the animal spirits came from that terrible moment with the bull.

Indeed, years later I thought back to that poor animal's awful death as a profound teaching in mercy and euthanasia. Particularly when I heard a respected religious teacher say that his cosmological fantasy insisted that people must at the end of their life continue suffering no matter how great the torment. He used as confirmation of such rigid mercilessness a quotation from distant scripture that even a broken-backed old horse dying in agony in the gutter with a crow pecking at its eyes should not be aided in its death.

Many, fearing the loss of a heaven they long ago felt they were unworthy of, somehow equate suffering with holiness. Not having resolved their personal guilt and grief, they still believe they deserve to suffer. And deny mercy to themselves and a world of pain so worthy of compassion calling out for surcease.

Skunk Satyagraha

About fifteen years ago, living amidst a world of wildlings in the forests of northern New Mexico, a few days after nestling in a few dozen chicks, I entered the coop one morning to find a dozen dead chicks with their heads bitten off. Skunks!

Recognizing too our responsibility to the skunks, in whose territory we had plopped a tantalizing chicken coop, rather than harming them, we began improving the fencing under which they had apparently entered. Digging all day along the fence line, we buried it well into the ground. Nothing short of a badger was going to dig its way into that enclosure. But the next morning more headless chicks.

We presumed the skunk had this time gone over rather than under the fence. It had seemingly climbed the chicken wire! We worked for most of the next day clumsily stretching sagging chicken wire across the top of the pen. When it was completed, we "knew" the few chicks remaining were at last safe. But next morning proved they were not. Somehow the predator was still getting in.

We had exhausted all our nonlethal options, but before taking more drastic measures, I decided to sit out one night in the well-fenced chicken yard in hopes of discovering the means of entrance.

After sitting outside in the cold for a few hours, I noticed that ego-glorifying self-righteous sense of wounded innocence slipping in. Self-interest-above-all was accumulating. Anger arising, animosity for this remarkably resourceful though deadly invasive creature. It was me against him. I considered what sort of buckshot to use. I was slipping into hunter identities. Catching my body hunching over, contracting like my mind, I spread wide my arms and arched my back to relieve the pressure. As my head tilted back, I looked up.

The enormous southwestern sky was wild with fiery asteroids. It was the Perseid meteor shower. A half-dozen streaks of light at a time stretched across the sky. Never had I seen such a full display. One after another and then five at a time, then crosswise another and another.

And wanting to rest my neck, I looked back down. And there, not ten feet in front of me, was the skunk. He had slipped through what seemed far too slight an aperture between the corner post and the fence.

He was as beautiful as anything in creation. For a long moment, bathed together in a surreal star shower, we looked deeply into each other's eyes. And beneath a singing sky we simultaneously bowed and retreated.

I returned with hammer and nails to secure the corner fencing. The skunk went home, and the sky kept on singing.

Teddy's Tub

When we were putting together our house in the woods, a carpenter friend asked if we would like an old oversized clawfoot bathtub. He was working on the remodeling of Bishop's Lodge, the once world-famous rest-and-relaxation destination of such notables as Theodore Roosevelt. In fact, he said the tub he was getting, being larger than most, might well have been used by the larger-than-most president.

When the tub came riding down the long dirt road in the back of his old pickup truck, we were not ready to install it, not yet having disassembled our old bathroom. We for the moment put it out behind the house on a slight rise under a favorite tree with a view all the way down the valley to the flat-topped volcano mountain in Abique just behind Georgia O'Keeffe's home and studio.

We put several throw pillows in the great antique tub so as to settle back and peruse the valley in great comfort. It was a great delight to our timber wolf Emmy, who after circling me would sometimes jump in the tub and dance in circles before snuggling down beside me.

Lounging in the tub one summer afternoon, I looked up and saw Ondrea flanked by Emmy, two Rottweilers, and our Saint Bernard running the ridge behind the house. Having just dislodged a couple of trespassing woodcutters, she was in fact that stunning woman who runs with wolves.

The tub now installed, sinking into the warm water in the midst of the Carson National Forest, I reflected on old Teddy perhaps sitting in this same tub almost a century before as he formulated the beginnings of the National Park System. Soon after, beginning with the consecration of Yellowstone.

When the Owl Calls Your Name, It's Your Turn in the Dentist's Chair

Another teaching from the animal spirits was recalled while I was waiting to have two extractions in the dentist's office. I remembered kneeling by the side of the road years before, unsuccessfully attempting to loosen the wing feathers of a dead great horned owl for an artful shamanic project. I pulled as hard as I could without crushing the feathers, but they would not budge. Then I was reminded of the Native American way, the original way of respect and interconnectedness with all creation. I stopped exerting such force on the long-flightless wing and instead respectfully asked its permission to remove the feathers. I bowed to it. When I tried again to extract the powerful feathers, they slipped effortlessly into my palm.

I gave permission to these two old teeth to go on their destined way, to let go. And so they did.

It is a beautiful morning. There is a lion on the mountainside behind the house. There is a lion in the heart behind the body.

The Mad-Raven Teachings

What do you do if the resident ravens fledge a full-grown child with some sort of brain anomaly that causes it to caw loudly about every three seconds—twenty times a minute—for weeks, sometimes quite near the house for hours, often outside your bedroom window at 5:30 A.M.?

One can feel the gut tighten when the mind notices the long repetition beginning once again. Then mindfulness softens from caw to caw.

In the course of reflecting on possible solutions, I recalled the experiment so many years ago in Japan in which the most sophisticated electroencephalograms measured brain reactions to long-repeated stimuli. The recurring ringing of a bell was noticed in the ordinary mind to slowly diminish in reaction as habituation to the stimuli occurred within a very few minutes. Ordinary subjects hardly noticed it after a while. But when advanced students of Zen, and even more so Zen Masters, were so measured, it was noticed that each time the bell was rung, no matter how many times, the same spiking of mindful response could be detected. They did not habituate, did not take bells or life for granted, and were completely nonresistant to each succeeding moment.

Could we use raven caw to bring us closer to the moment instead of following the ordinary aversion to uncontrollable, even unpleasant repetition?

Often when quiet and present, we could receive the sound with no aversion and even a considerable concern for its well-being. But often when focused elsewhere, we found it an unwelcome intrusion.

But what at first was resisted by fear and aversion was gradually surrendered into with mercy and awareness. Like any healing, when what turned to suffering is revealed and entered, the long abandoned is called home.

Even now I hear our poor brain-damaged ward down the valley heading this way.

We thought a few months ago when we first heard the long calling that the bird would probably die soon from whatever birth defect had caused its unusual behavior.

And here it comes now, calling out in its own way, *"Karuna, Karuna"* ("Compassion, compassion") as did Huxley's birds in his

Island. And, settling on a nearby branch, it echoes those long-lost birds, "Here and Now Boys! Here and Now!"

Reminding us to soften. And that some questions, particularly those that deal directly with life, have no answer. That sometimes even love can't readily find a way.

Never was the need for surrender clearer or the fact that to honor the Buddha is to wash the feet of all sentient beings.

(The Tao of things never ceases to amaze me. Soon after writing the above, after nearly three months of experiencing the full range of emotion from frustrated reaction to heartfelt response, our obsessive-compulsive young raven disappeared from the valley. He was an excellent teacher.)

Does the Buddha Have Cat Nature?

The cat looks into the mirror leaning against the wall. She sees the face of a cat, her face, and reaches behind the glass to touch who's there. But there is nothing, no one, only a flat image staring back.

And she too learns what the Chinese Master said, that "what we are looking for is that which is looking."

Cats have Buddha nature too. It's not just dogs and foxes—no canine bigots in the Pure Land—she purrs MU.

the mystery that includes pain, sickness, old age, and death

THIRTY-FOUR

impermanence

Buddha spoke of the importance of comprehending the inevitability of pain, sickness, old age, and death, of the truth of impermanence.

Impermanence is the bane and blessing of our lives. It brings love and takes it away. It brings birth as readily as death. If it were not for impermanence, there would be no growth. And nothing to remind us of what lies beyond.

In the Mahalila, the Great Dance, the Vaudeville of Impermanence, which swings between life and death, in a flash history disappears and a deeper truth than time emerges.

Even for the aged monk slumped lifeless against the forest tree, even for the murderer strapped in the execution chamber, things can and will change.

At the very center of impermanence there is an Unmoving that never changes. It is our deeper-than-nature nature. It is even before we were unborn, before even our faceless face. It is the ether of formlessness.

We are a momentary convergence.

When Siddhartha first went beyond his palace walls, it was his unprecedented contact with pain, sickness, old age, and death that caused his awakening. Perhaps he thought he would never age or die. But when he saw the truth of impermanence, it displaced the marrow in his bones, and he turned to look the mystery dead in the eye.

When the Buddha-to-be left the palace, it was on the trembling ground of impermanence that he rode forth to discover in time the timeless.

Energy unfolds as incessant change. Consciousness flows. What changes one thought into the next moves the stars across the sky.

When asked how anyone could be happy or even satisfied in a world constantly in unpredictable, uncontrollable transition, the Buddhist meditation master Achan Cha held up a crystal goblet and asked the assembly to look at the beautiful object that had been given him earlier in the day, to see how a little rainbow splayed out across the water. The crystal made such a wonderful clear sound when it was tapped.

But he said he knew this glass was already broken. So when the wind blew it from a shelf or his elbow brushed it from the table he could look down at its new form of a thousand pieces and admire that too, knowing that form also would not last.

He could be content because he cherished the fleeting moment from at least a momentary unbroken presence.

Clearing brush the evening before a ten-day meditation retreat, I spattered my arms and face with poison oak.

It was not until after the retreat began that its extent was realized.

As my face and arms began to turn red and blister, as an experiment in consciousness, I made a vow, took a *tapasaya* (a Hindu term for using difficulties as a means of strengthening practice), not to scratch.

At night, so as not to involuntarily scratch, I slept with my arms extended above my head like one surrendering. My old corpse-sleep meditation was coming in very handy. Any movement immediately triggered my alarm.

Before the next day had passed, my eyes were nearly closed from facial swelling.

At times, when my mindfulness lagged, the compulsion to relieve discomfort started making a very strong case. While on my cushion, my foot would rise off the floor of its own mercy and try to rub my fiery wrist and forearm. I had to just say no.

After another day my face and arms were swollen and crusty. In order not to move involuntarily, there was the absolute necessity to maintain moment-to-moment awareness, to stay absolutely present.

My concentration rarely better.

After a few days of not scratching and sending clear mercy into my sizzling skin, my desire for that particular experiment in consciousness was sated. And before my eyes were completely swollen shut, I left the retreat for the afternoon to get a cortisone shot.

As I drove to the doctor's office, the trees were melting. The shafts of sunlight through the undulating redwoods yet more solid than the road before me. Everything composing and decomposing moment to moment. Even thoughts unable to stay but an instant before melting. Everything dying and arising completely anew from millisecond to millisecond. It was a classic opening of the doors of perception.

Perception had expanded from fifteen frames a second to several times that number. Slow-motion seeing speeding up everything. Matter constantly dissolving. Reality revealing the slippery underlying nature of creation.

Returning a few hours later to my meditation, thankful to the bovine sacrifice that provides cortisone, as I settled in, pulled back from forgetting, I noticed that my fascinating seeing had abated. And that big laugh saying, "Even impermanence is impermanent; remember that when you're dying."

Passing beneath ordinary consciousness, as with the shaking loose of ego stasis, we feel more like a stream than an island, more a process unfolding than anything I could hang my hat on.

Nouns lie about time. We are constantly becoming something else. Ignorance and enlightenment are equidistant from our next step.

A table or a chair is just that for a cosmic moment until wood mites and the wind turn it to sawdust and the momentum some call evolution and others refer to as karma continues turning it to soil, turning it to wood, turning it to chair once again a cosmic moment later.

We never return to a room exactly the same person who left, and it is never the same room.

As the heart whispers to the thousands of aspirants silently observing their unfolding process in a thousand meditation halls and monasteries, "Mind is big sky changing."

THIRTY-FIVE

pain and sickness

At nineteen, the injury to my lower back from the previous summer's work in the steel mill caused me progressive limitation in movement and a gradual increase in physical discomfort. Back at school in Miami, playing drums with the band became increasingly difficult. Unable to easily stand once I'd sat down, I saved the ordeal of getting back up until the end of the night and did not leave the bandstand during the breaks between sets, just turning my stool so my back was to the drums. Having increasing difficulty putting my foot down on the clutch, I knew it was time to do something about the gradually sharper pain and lack of mobility.

After the two ruptured lumbar disks were removed, I could at last work and travel again. And headed toward the long introspection of Buddha's Garage.

But over the years the pain in my sciatic nerve reestablished itself. The neurologist I conferred with ten years after the operation said that such tightening adhesions were quite common and that, in fact, 40 percent of these procedures had to be redone.

"You'll just have to learn to live with the pain!" he said. Always good advice of course, but also an inspiration, a challenge to the mind to sink into the heart. Pain became a reminder, almost an inspiration, to soften the long-conditioned hard reaction to the unpleasant. To enter with mercy those parts of myself, mental as well as physical, that I had withdrawn from in fear and judgment.

The rare lumbar spasms over the years became quite workable and a particularly useful test and proof of the guided pain and healing meditations we were sharing with so many. Softening around and focusing a merciful, even loving, awareness inside the area of discomfort.

Maharaji used to say that he loved hospitals and graveyards because it brought the God out in people. I found that pain acts in a similar manner, calling forth mindfulness and mercy. Offering time and again a very direct feedback for my states of mind and body. Even a sense of the many beside myself experiencing this same pain in this shared body. It taught me an almost devotional quality of quiet and tenderness for our shared pain.

I was learning how deep love might go even in difficult situations and how powerful an ever softening mindfulness could become when a merciful awareness opened to it all. As one teacher reminded me when I mentioned that pain was teaching me to open my heart in hell, "We must go beyond heaven and hell to love ourselves when we are in pain; otherwise we will just be pretending all the rest of the time."

About twenty years ago when I was forty-five, three more disks began to collapse in my neck. I switched from my long-accustomed meditation bench to a *zafu*, a meditation cushion.

The not so secret teachings continued. I stopped driving. I switched to meditating in an upholstered chair. As the teachings say, the real test of practice is pain and fatigue. Sometimes I passed the test; sometimes I only had room for one breath at a time and all bets were off.

In those difficult moments I was reminded of an old friend whom, when he was dying, I asked if he wanted to meditate. He said he didn't want his mind expanded because he had his hands full with it the size it was. And my love for him touched my pain too.

But, as I was discovering, the pain didn't have to change in size, only the space it was floating in. As the Zen Master advised, give a wild horse a big pasture and it will roll in the grass and chase butterflies, but confine that restless being to a small stall and it will kick out the slats and become very difficult to approach.

The heart had to continually encourage the mind not to sink into some self-pitying identification with the pain, which turned it to suffering.

It was evident that if you have a body, if you have a mind, you will have pain.

That physical pain was due to sensations too large to pass effortlessly through the nerve net of the body.

But that mental pain was due to the absence of a deeper truth.

Pain reminded me there was more to heal than I knew hurt. When I touched my pain, the pain, with fear, there was pity, but when I received it with mercy there was compassion.

When I saw it as my pain alone, I experienced self-pity, I shrank to grief. But when I recognized it as the pain we all share, I expanded into something universal.

It was clear that, despite what pain repeatedly suggested, I was not simply that; neither body nor mind.

The oft-repeated concept the we are responsible for our illnesses, for our pain, is more mind than heart. We are not responsible *for* our illness; we are responsible *to* our illness. Responsible *for* pain is guilt and grief. Responsible *to* it is love.

Responsibility is not blame. It is the ability to respond rather than the compulsive need to react. The tendency of mindfulness to displace compulsivity. Responding with a merciful awareness allows pain to remain out in the open where it is accessible to healing.

In the light of awareness, mental and physical pain have less of a tendency to become identified with, or endemic to, our personal myth.

Some, such as that old monk who thought that people, like that dying horse, should suffer to the end, think suffering is somehow noble, that pain is holy. I have seen all too many Judgment Day–fearing people dying in great pain because of this hopeful, tortured self-negation.

There is nothing holy about pain. We need to stop deifying our suffering!

Pain becomes suffering as we harden to it. Softening is such relief, such grace to just sit lovingly with a modicum of discomfort, remembering all those others at this moment with this same pain in this same body of pain and compassion.

When we keep our pain close to our heart, there arises insight and even compassion. There is a healing when what we fear is warmly received in a clear awareness.

When the work with our lesser pains leads to the access and healing of our greater pains, there is the potential for grace. Grace being, by one definition, that which takes us closer to our true nature; and from another point of view grace *is* our true nature.

When I worked most closely with dying children, I would often find myself praying that this great pain be relieved from such small bodies.

Sitting next to fifteen-month-old Sara, whose cancer had begun in the womb, as she received a long chemotherapy infusion, I felt my prayer abruptly interrupted. It was almost as though a warm blanket had been thrown over me to halt my continued unskillful wishfulness. And the heart said, "Stop! You're just second-guessing God. You don't know enough to make that prayer. The only appropriate prayer is, 'May you get the most out of this possible.'"

It changed how I dealt with my and others' pain. It replaced urgency and judgment with trust in the process. It decreased the fatigue of resistance. It deepened confidence in even unlikely intuitions. It was a step closer to dissolving the separation between the healer and the healing.

Pain, though, does have its benefits. As the Dalai Lama has pointed out, if it were not for pain, there would be no compassion. Pain draws compassion like its opposite, stillness, draws wisdom.

Pain also attracts grief. Both the unresolved loss of loved ones as well as our wearying, everyday, ordinary grief. The insistent lamentation of our wounded sense of self enunciates itself the closer to pain we get.

Perhaps around physical pain is noticed mental pain: doubt, fear, anger, even remorse. Momentary pain calls longtime suffering out of the woodwork.

Fifteen minutes of acute pain can uncover a lifetime of chronic discomfort.

As mercy gradually infuses the space in which pain floats, great relief may be found. And unexpected levels of healing exposed.

Pain does not cry out only for the absence of pain. It calls for a peace in which not only this hurt, but all hurt, might be met with mercy rather than fear, with kindness and clarity.

There was something within pain that counseled me to be merciful. It displayed how hard I was on myself. And how rarely I touched my pain, anyone's pain, with kindness. It defined healing as mercy and awareness as it entered those areas of the mind and body from which I had fearfully withdrawn.

When we soften around pain, the armoring about the heart begins to melt and the resistance that converts pain to suffering diminishes.

Freud said neurosis is a refusal to suffer. Though he rarely acknowledged the mystery, he, like a thousand Buddhist meditation masters, reminds us of the pain that ends pain. The somewhat painful opening to our long-imprisoned wounds. Exposing the condition beneath the pain, which supports and maintains suffering, to the healing light of a merciful awareness.

Nothing turns pain to suffering like anger. Conditioning sends aversion, even disgust, into the stubbed toe and we tighten.

We have forgotten compassion when it is most called for. We curse the stubbed toe, we go deaf to its pleas for mercy. We harden to it, we send hatred into it. Even the most peace-loving persons may think cruelly of pain and aggressively push some part of themselves away when in greatest need.

But remembering the heart, we can soften and let the sensations emanating from the stubbed toe dissipate like the fading sparks of a roman candle descending through deep space.

We can send blessing instead of fear into the pain and turn toward the throbbing, as toward the mystery, with openness and clear intention.

Not knowing what might come next, trusting the process, listening in a gradually deepening silence, in our hearts we hear, "May you get the most out of this possible."

THIRTY-SIX

aging and old age

In the fall of 2000 Jack Kornfield invited me to be on a panel at the Western Buddhist Teachers Conference to be held at the Spirit Rock Meditation Center. It would be a discussion group with a number of meditation teachers including the Dalai Lama. When I asked what he wanted me to give a talk about in such august company, he replied, "Aging."

"Who me? Aging? Ah, yes, me aging!"

"Even some of the most developed still have not quite tuned to their aging," he said.

Though it seemed unlikely I would be able to attend, it did remind me that the ghost of my childhood had long since grayed setting up housekeeping under the banyan tree.

Everything is aging. Even the idea of entropy is getting kind of old.

Chogyam Trungpa said meditation is just one insult after another. One false idol after another torn down for use as building materials. Aging too can be one insult after another if we hope to maintain that self-image which has always caused such discomfort. Unfinished business raises our blood pressure and lowers our self-esteem.

Or it can be one insight after another, one more opening toward peace.

Once during an extended meditation retreat on my thirty-sixth birthday, I returned to my room to find a note on my pillow that read, "May this be your last birthday!" Dharma sister and now widely respected teacher Julie Wester had left me the greatest of blessings: an opportunity to let go another level deeper. To not celebrate myself too shallow. To not imagine I was just time in a body and forget my great unborn nature. And the sooner I got truly born, the better!

Aging is a process of gestation, a spiritual option. It is not a slow death, but a crucial part of our unending birth. Though the body may be getting a bit loose on the bone, the heart can be like a mountain growing less distant each day.

Though you were born as the heavy body so many years ago and are still complaining about gravity, let go of the hungry ghost of disappointment. Some say it was born at the first removal from the breast and has grown with each not-getting ever since. Try something lighter than the ordinary grief by which we have falteringly navigated throughout life.

We have seen those who took "the opportunity to age" as a spiritual endeavor, sharing through service to others these precious years of growth and love. Some by way of prayer for the benefit of many. Some through child care for neighbors, or via the Internet in "chat groups of the soul." And some each morning simply looking into their heart as though it were a crystal ball and asking, "What's good for today?"

Aging is the chance of a lifetime!

In the process of aging, the energy of the body gradually withdraws into the heart. For this reason, spiritual work in the later years can often be the most productive of one's life. The spirit is more accessible in this great indwelling than perhaps at any other time. Lightenment has never been so available.

Much of the death scenario, of the calm that follows the storm, can be explored long before death by the keen inner eye of one who appreciates the day-to-day accumulation at the center of the chest.

In the process we call dying, when the body can no longer contain it, the life force withdraws into the heart, collecting rapidly there.

In dying the life force recedes into the heart and departs through the top of the head. When in aging, as in dying, the body can no longer support it, there is a gathering of the life energy in the heart, which, it is said, as death approaches, rises like a fountain from the crown of the skull.

Aging mirrors this process in a very useful and beneficial manner. We have repeatedly observed this great drawing in of energy, which completes the heart, in patients whose life eventually dissolved into the Great Satisfaction with their last breath.

In aging a gradual, rather than rapid, accumulation of the light in the light chamber gives rise to a sense of even greater aliveness.

I have heard many in advanced years, illuminated by this ingathering and concentration of the life force, remark that though they may have been seventy-five, they felt like they were sixteen at heart. I have, however, rarely heard forty-year-olds say they feel sixteen—more often they say they feel sixty-five.

There is a pulling at our heart by the wonderful teachings of Dr. Joan Borysenko, who with extraordinary clarity brings up a most fascinating reality—that as we advance in age we change sexes somewhat.

Men take on many of the secondary sexual characteristics of women, such as a decrease in muscle mass and an increase in breast mass. Just as women present more male characteristics, such as a decrease of long luxurious hair on the top of the skull and an increase in facial hair on the front.

It is a wisdom time.

After the wearying metamorphosis of menopause women may opt for a freedom that draws on their active, self-possessed, creative, yang, societal male-associated tendencies and brings great satisfaction. And even a glimpse of the Great Satisfaction on occasion.

A woman's role may change from identification with the small family to joining in the strength of the greater family.

When people retire and wonder, "If I'm not my job, then who the hell am I?" they are getting close to the reason they were born. They are beginning to inquire into the being behind all their doing and becoming. Indeed, many do not ask themselves the question they were born to ask until the shadows lengthen. But it's never too late to be born. It's never inappropriate to ask, "Who am I?

"Now that my familial and social responsibilities are completed, now that the identities for which I was praised are no longer my day, who am I?"

If I'm not a salesman (no job), or a parent (children long gone), or a model (cultural concepts of beauty), or a pickpocket (arthritis), then who am I? And since I'm asking, "Who am I?" I'd like to ask yet a bit deeper, "Who am I really?"

Who was I before what I became? And before that?

I met a longtime student of an aging teacher who was beginning to demonstrate a bit of organic brain syndrome. His teacher was forgetting the teachings. So he returned the gift beyond measure, which were his teacher's teachings, to his teacher. He taught as he had been taught. The love in that room!

He had been taught that the mind creates the abyss and the heart crosses it. He had been taught that love is the bridge. And so he carried supplies daily over that bridge.

His teacher, who had so loved the timeless, had now lost time.

His teacher said, "Now there are no days, no weeks, or months for me. No seasons, no years . . . I have to pull to get back into time."

Having crossed an ocean of resistance and attachment, now residing in this timelessness, his love is even greater than before. "Now the heart is so full, the body has to fit in where it can." He is no longer rational, but never irrational. He lives now where love is more than a thought and each thought refers back to the heart. Love is not his state of mind, but his state of being.

Father Bede Griffith, a spiritual seeker throughout his remarkable life, said he learned more in the last two years of his life than he did in the first eighty-four.

I recently heard an interesting idea about the aging of the body: that it is an allergic reaction.

Waking from deep sleep with a great need for a bathroom. The room pitch black. Stumbling in a dream daze, I cannot find the door out of our bedroom.

The plants are against the wrong wall, clothes hanging where a window should be, the bed gone north . . . I am completely disoriented and desperate to find a toilet . . .

I am an old man lost in his own home.

I am the brain hardening, shrinking.

I am the process at the far end of creation, Shiva's left-handed dance, that which comes before and after the beginning and end of the world.

As I call out in the dark, Ondrea turns on the light and I am temporarily pulled back from inevitable decay.

IN MEMORY OF . . . WHAT WAS THAT AGAIN?

A few years ago, when he was quite old and rather frail, I heard Krishnamurti address a large assembly.

He spoke with his accustomed softness and care for a few minutes before calling on a fellow who had raised his hand with a question. Krishnamurti answered slowly, then stopped and began again, then stopped again. He said his aging had caused him to not always be so very sharp and would the fellow just come down and hold his hand.

It was a teaching for us all that some day all that might be left of us is our love.

Buddha indicated that knowing where you are is more important than knowing where you are going.

We don't need a compass or even a road map. All we need is the heart to take one step at a time.

When asked directions, the Zen Master often repeated, "Just go straight!" Present moment to moment, not thinking backward or forward.

One of the great teachings of aging and the alteration of memory is learning to be wrong.

We act as though being wrong is a sin, a slight against heaven, a step toward perdition.

Ah, mistaken again!

It is time, indeed, for us to learn to be in error, to be responsible, to let go of too little and too much.

We have been right for so long, we have forgotten how to be completely honest. It took us so many sleights of hand and heart to appear worthy.

Now, on occasion corrected, I am delighted to watch my heart remain open to a truth other than the one to which I might previously have held so tightly.

I am slowly learning to be wrong. It is a great relief!

"To be truly present," as Achan Cha, a respected guide, put it, "all you have to remember is *just this much!*" Holding his thumb and index finger apart about the length a spark might jump, just this much, just this eternal instant, just the living truth!

When memory falters, we are forced back into the living present, where life is to be lived. The past is irretrievably departed, only this morning's sun, only that love across the table. *Just this much* remains.

It is said if you can stay aware of just this much, just this frame of the inner movie, just one moment at a time of the passing show, you will find what you are looking for.

But what, the fearing mind asks, if it gets difficult to remember even "just this much"? What if I forget where I'm going or where I've been?

After a workshop in which these questions arose, a woman took me aside to say she had tended most of the members of her family during their decline from Alzheimer's disease. Most of her life had been dedicated to caring for parents and siblings progressively affected by, as she put it, "their lost mind." And now, just as she was about to go out into the world unencumbered by such responsibility, she noticed familiar symptoms. She was heartbroken and angry.

"I'm not going to go through that long deterioration with no one to help me like I was there for my mother and sisters. Damn it, just as I was about to get my life back!"

She said she would just as well be dead as deteriorate in some forgotten corner of the county hospital. "In fact," she said, "this is probably the last time you'll see me at a workshop. Thanks."

We spoke for a few minutes about the new freedom available to her, how mild her symptoms were so far, and how in a way this could be one of the most creative periods in her life. And whatever she finally decided to do about dealing with the degenerative process, she had time on her side.

She said she would not rush into anything and would consider her options. But by no means was she going to spend the next seven or ten years dying confused, frightened, and alone!

We were pleasantly surprised to see her eight months later. She seemed only slightly affected by her family's genetic legacy. "So far so good, and life is good."

When we inquired how she had dealt with those suicidal feelings, she told us that she had put the "blue pills" in her mother's favorite crystal goblet and placed it on the mantelpiece. Next to it she said she put a neatly written note that said, "If you don't know what these pills are for, take them!"

She lived until she died.

When we remember our true home, we rarely get lost in quite the same old way. All we have to remember is just this much.

Forgetful Buddha says, "At times I may even forget I am forgetful, but I never forget I am Buddha."

THIRTY-SEVEN

death

Just because we never die doesn't mean you'll live forever.

A discussion from God knows where with God knows who:

Receiving an anxious phone call from a physician friend who had just completed diagnostic blood tests, I was told (mistakenly) that there were serious if not fatal difficulties with my liver. Having had hepatitis in my needle days, I presumed that was the cause. It was suggested that I go to the hospital. He would make arrangements and call back within the hour.

Sometimes we just can't get out of death's way and must open to the possibility that today we might leave this life behind and go on to the next.

Waiting for the return call, I turned to what in my heart represents Maharaji to share the fear that I might die. Anticipating magnanimous pity and condolences, I heard the old trickster, smiling more warmly than ever, instead say, "Good. I miss you!" It certainly was not what I was expecting.

But the increasingly present voice within said not to take such a dual-istic reply at face value. "Well, then, take it at Original Face value. No one dies much, and never separate from how they love is what remains."

I was enveloped in the overwhelming compassion of Maharaji's love.

The phone rang and the test results were botched at the lab and the doctor was sorry and he was glad and stay healthy good-bye.

Some people take longer to die than others.

Hitler and Jesus are on TV daily.

Elvis is still seen eating ribs at the end of a dirt road in Milwaukee.

The dear ones of our youth, kind friends, and candlelit lovers sit on their graves, not in them.

Our parents die the slowest. Our children the slowest yet.

Shakespeare said, "The good men do is interred with their bones." But the ocean carries us all, light or heavy, eventually to the Other Shore. The tides gradually erase everything but love and hate. These two keep us in our heaven or hell and foretell our birth, or at least our mood upon rising.

There are many variations on the theme of what the mystery might be, but no one, I suspect, would disagree that to understand death would be to have a major piece in the puzzle.

Last year, every once in a while just as I was about to doze off, two or three breaths into sleep, the breath stopped. Still somewhat aware of it, I'd struggled to the surface gasping like one long under water. I awoke shaken as though almost buried alive.

With absolutely no control and no resources to escape, there was nothing there but fear in space.

It was clearly up to me which to choose, fear or the vast spaciousness it was floating in.

One of those terrible/wonderful opportunities to play our edge.

Awakened by sleep apnea as from the condition of sleep paralysis,
which a few patients have frighteningly described, I share a moment
with those confused and disoriented in their beds, wondering if they
are dying. And another room is opened in His mansion . . . and the
healing family expands.

And as distinctly unpleasant as it was, I find something in me looking forward to the next distressing occasion.

It was a rare opportunity to follow the repeated suggestion of the
mystery, Plato, and the Dalai Lama to "practice dying."

Indeed, there is a major aspect of the dharma that focuses on
preparing for death. In this regard, as mentioned to the Dalai Lama,
based on his comments, we devised a year-to-year practice for those
drawn to such an experiment in consciousness.

Many groups around the country formed for the exploration of unfinished business while cultivating a mindfulness and loving-kindness
meditation practice. Indeed, the book you are reading is partially the
result of the intense life-review process called for in this experiment in
consciousness.

THE MYSTERY REVEALS ITSELF

When the mystery reveals itself, what is exposed seems already so
deeply known. Yet you are overwhelmed with humility and gratitude.

There is a moment on passing into death when the psyche calls out
for every last molecule of oxygen to stay just one more moment, one
more breath, in the body. Our whole consciousness is focused on staying in the body. We would do anything, but we can't. There is the
thought of struggle, but the muscles do not respond. Momentary fear
melts into unexpected quiet.

For a moment the breath seems not full or empty, but just still.

The element of solidity is falling away. To those about you it seems that the unmistakable marker of death, the body's inability to move, the beginning of rigor, has overtaken it.

But from within a remarkable lightness seems to arise. In fact, exactly the opposite of the predominance of solidity in the dead body is encountered as a freedom from solidity is experienced within.

In that stillness, in that space between breaths, between thoughts, between lives, something is suddenly remembered. Something it seems impossible to ever have forgotten. You glimpse your unborn, undying essence and realize that staying any longer in the body does not satisfy your deepest longing. The evolutionary momentum, the will toward mystery, to be completed.

You are less sure why you were fighting for the body. And all resistance vanishes.

There suffuses a boundless luminosity that draws the heart forward as it surrenders the body into death.

The awareness departing the body remembers with enormous joy who it really is.

As we pass through this "point of remembrance," it becomes clear, as it is said, that we were not human beings having a spiritual experience, but spiritual beings having a human experience.

Passing through that portal, which begins to reconnect us with our greatest selves, our perspective on life changes. There is great gratitude and relief. Beyond all worldly reason we see how perfect a teaching even death might be and how meticulously creative is the process of our growth.

The uncoupling that frees the spirit from the body continuing as the outer signs of the "closing down of the body" are increasingly accompanied within by a feeling of expansion and a sense of rising.

To the bystander the unmistakable signatures of death are the hardening and cooling of the body, but within, as the heat leaves the body, there is a sensation like the radiant energy seen rising from a macadam road in summer. A radiating outward. A sense of lightness. A feeling of dissolving upward into the enormity.

The individual's sense of dying, of dropping the body, of shedding level after level of form parallels the melting of an ice cube. As heat escapes, the frozen mass loses its solid form, shape-shifting from hard edge to the fluid boundaries of a puddle. Surrendering up its separate heat, it merges into the greater whole, "becoming room temperature." As consciousness continues to become less "centrally located," it becomes boundaryless and disperses like the evaporated cube "equally in all its parts." Disappeared into thin air and yet a greater sense of spaciousness.

And through all these remarkable changes from solidity to invisibility, that ice cube has not changed in essence in the least. It is still absolutely H_2O! Wholly unaffected by any form it might take on in the process.

The dimensions of the process of dying, indeed of the universe itself, changed as more was revealed over the years in the course of the meditative investigations that originally displayed the point of remembrance.

Rising through the joy of remembering our deathless essence, the heart continued to expand until all lesser leanings fell away, and my only priority was love.

In every fiber of my being I understood that love was the only rational act of a lifetime. And with some dismay I perceived how everything else, how anything else, was just a lot of nonsense and folderol.

We may have always thought of ourselves as loving persons, but when we look back at our lives with *only* love as the measure, we become weak in what used to be our knees. So many other qualities clearly held precedence over love. So much done under the guise of survival and the imperative to elude pain. More desirous of love than offering it, following so many desires down so many dark alleys. So many dead ends. And all that was said and done because we thought we were right or were sure they were wrong.

Taken by the flow into the arduous healing in which nothing matters but love, I could see that it was at this point in the process of dying that many had fearfully mythologized concepts such as Judgment Day.

There is no judgment from on high on Judgment Day, but only our own discomfort when we look back at how shallowly we sometimes lived our lives. Love is agonized by how rarely kindness and mercy took precedence over the personal hungers that now seem so trivial.

All the times we manipulated the world instead of serving it, inexcusable to the priority of love.

All the moments when another person was just an object in our mind rather than the subject of our heart. All the times we feigned love to get what was not given. All the stolen emotions. All the times of fear and forgetfulness.

It is a moment where the heart and mind might collide. But if the heart can abide just a moment longer, if a lifetime of remembering offers us just one more moment of remembering, it catches a glimpse of itself in the mirror of mindfulness, and another level of insight arises. Watching what at first seems to be the inescapable suffering caused by not living in a wholly loving manner, we notice something very subtle, a shadow of the hungry ghost flitting by.

In what momentarily passed for Judgment Day, there is noticed a powerful element of illusion, even delusion, when it is recognized that it is not just the absence of love that is causing all this pain but the presence of unyielding attachment. It is not love that judges but the models of perfection to which we cling. Indeed, as we pass through this necessary mirage it becomes apparent that perfection is incapable of seeing perfection. It is a very subtle teaching at first, but one worth going through hell to discover.

Judging everything against love is not the same as seeing with the eyes of love. Actually it is the effect of not perceiving in that manner.

When we see more fully with the eyes of love, there is of course no judgment. And mercy mends the fissures on the surface of the heart.

Though we may be momentarily shocked by how many times we missed the mark and lost an opportunity to heal ourselves and others, the teaching is clear. That love is the highest form of acceptance and judgment is not, will not, cannot.

When we recognize the injury we have done because our priority was so often the defense of the wounded sense of self, another level is revealed. A level that has no priorities, only the natural momentum of the heart dissolving like a lump of sugar into the Ocean of Being.

No priorities even of love, for only love will do.

There is no judgment but our own. No high priest to question us at the gate. There is only the distance between the heart and mind to be traversed as we are drawn toward our great light, what the Tibetans refer to as the *dharmata,* the fiery hoop of the Great Spirit through which we enter into the eternal mystery.

When diagnosed with a profoundly degenerative disease, a patient said he'd die before he would let himself become a vegetable.

As the illness progressed, he said he would kill himself when he could no longer "clean my own bottom." When that day came, it was sunny, and still he was getting so much love from life he said he'd stay until he could no longer feed himself. When that day came, though his body was a wreck, his heart was still intact and he said he'd stay a while longer until he could no longer sleep lying down.

He could not leave life, he said, because it was too beautiful. "Just being is enough!" he murmured.

He died sitting in his sleep. Although many about him feared dying in so slow and difficult a manner, I think they feared more not being able to live as wholeheartedly as he.

The yoga conference auditorium was about half full when Ondrea and I arrived for our keynote talk.

As the room continued to fill with yoga instructors, it was noted with a soft laugh that it looked like "a healthier crowd than usual." Most of our groups had at least a few terminal patients and exhausted caregivers.

As the talk began, the group seemed focused and receptive. Concepts about the enormity of our deathless Great Nature were greeted with obvious appreciation.

But when we said that, although we live forever, it doesn't mean you'll never die, a noticeable chill seemed to spread across the room.

When we said, "Who you really are never dies, but who you appear to be can't keep up appearances forever!" sphincters in the room could be heard snapping shut.

Speaking to the issue of clinging to the body as a source of suffering when I said, "You are not the body," a wave of restlessness passed through the audience. A noticeable discomfort seemed to arise as we spoke of our true nature needing nothing, not even a body, to be whole.

Slowly the back rows began to stand and saunter out.

By the time we got to, "We think we need the body to exist, but it's just the other way around; the body needs us for its existence, and when we depart, it displays its true nature as rotting meat and a disposal problem," they were pushing in line to get out of the room. Perhaps two hundred and fifty people, half the audience, left.

It was a remarkable experience for Ondrea and me to watch dozens at a time rush for the exits. Ego was standing at attention watching itself watch such abandonment.

Then it became clear: the motivation for a sizable amount of the yoga practice in that room was to increase longevity and enhance appearance. They did not want to hear about not being a body. They wanted to know how to hold on to that body as long as possible.

I must admit we laughed a bit after the event when we imagined how horrified they must have been. Worse than death is the fear of death.

THIRTY-EIGHT

afterlife, afterdeath

A Buddhist friend said, "It's not hard to die. It's just hard to stay dead."

Though the concept of reincarnation was always tempting, I, so colorful of ego, was never able to wholly endorse it because I could not imagine being anyone else.

I could not "feel" myself in any other time or place. I was so much me, how could I ever be someone else?!

Sitting on the floor between my children's beds perhaps twenty-eight years ago waiting for them to get home from school one day, feeling very much my role as father, *their* father, a bit of intuitive insight floated by that made clear how strongly my identification with old roles resisted the idea of reincarnation.

A different feeling than "me right to the core" presented itself. For a quiet moment I saw that what I was thinking of as the eternal Steve was just a batch of conditioning and some short story that my great grandfather had begun to tell and that I might finish if I've got the heart.

Once again, at yet another level, the liberating teaching of "No one to be, nowhere to go, nothing to do."

What I called my self wasn't mine after all. Just another ceremonial mask. Another lifetime to be concealed beneath. That what peered through the eye slots, that what was looking, was what we really were. And then I could see myself simply as spirit in any time in any place in any guise.

Behind who we think we are is something fearless. Behind who we imagine ourselves to be is our legacy. Behind thinking is who we are before we become lost in thought. Our center of gravity is constantly changing.

We mutate with the shifting light. Our orbit is constantly expanding. We are the momentary result of incessant change.

It is said that we literally cannot be who or what we wish to be, because even when we see who we wish to be pass through, and proudly evince as many of its characteristics as we can, the pride itself and all the other bits of self-concerned flotsam can conjure the next pretense, the next mood, the next forgetfulness, the next incarnation.

When people speak of reincarnation, they are often referring to some vague idea of a soul-object passing from one body to another.

Few realize the essence never takes birth, never takes death, but simply observes all this, unless, as is commonly the case, lost or obscured in small identities.

But when we speak of death and particularly afterdeath, superstitions rise from their graves to attempt to control the uncontrollable unfolding of impermanence.

One of the few common areas of agreement about the nature of the soul is that when we die (whether eternal or just long-lasting), it ascends from the body. The trick of course is, no matter what you believe, to ascend with it!

Or as my old friend Wavy Gravy used to say to dying children in the hospital, "If the light goes left, go left. If the light goes right, go right."

We do not simply "take" a human birth; we commit eons to shaking loose the fierce grasping and cold indifference of the hungry ghost, becoming truly human through repeated births and deaths.

A human incarnation may be composed of many births and last thousands of years before the transformation is complete. And pilgrimage into the next form of consciousness is undertaken.

When we have finished with unfinished business, both personally and conceptually, when we are completely born, it is said we will no longer require a human body for a schoolroom. As the teachings get subtler, we inhabit subtler bodies, I am told.

Only one question could be asked of the Buddhist meditation master who was an authority on *annapana*, the basic mindfulness-of-breathing technique. So, wondering aloud if there was still a field of sensation after you leave the body, if there might be some subtle energy pulsation akin to sensation in the lighter body, I asked, "Can we watch our breath after we die?"

The translator's eyebrows arched like the hands of a martial artist. Clearing his throat, he inquired if I was certain that was the question I wished to ask. Encouraged by his loss of countenance, I assured him that the continuance of the experience of sensation was indeed the information I was seeking. He reluctantly passed the question to the teacher, who frowned and brushed it away with a beautifully simple gesture.

His particular sect, unlike most other schools of Buddhist thought, did not entertain the idea of an interstice between lives. Our last breath here, according to his scriptures, was followed immediately by our first breath in the next body. A hardworking bunch this lineage, no time for rest and relaxation, no time for healing and integration, no time for the timeless.

The question, he felt, was not worth considering.

But it was a very simple question:

When the planets stop spinning, when gravity ceases in the stone garden, when the spirit floats free and there you are, how does it feel?

Now is that too much to ask?

And I wonder if he would shrug off that same question now, dead as he's been for the past few years.

Does the field of sensation disappear with the body or does the lighter body experience yet lighter sensation?

Some say sensation is transposed into sound. The celestial choir where the nerve ends used to be. Where once was the field of sensation, the sixty-four thousand celestial serpents of the nerve currents arch above us, their shining cobra hoods expanded to shelter and encourage us as we enter, luminous, the deathless field of being.

I dreamed last night of being dead with old friends. Sitting comfortably in what seemed a well-appointed country club. Conversing together from the wider perspective that demagnetizes suffering. Leaving one by one through the door that led to new birth, we bid each other adieu.

Leaving the dream, I turned to say, "I guess we won't recognize each other the next time we meet, but I hope we love as well as we do right now."

pilgrim's progress

big self surprise party

Sometimes the top of the head opens before the rest of the body is ready.

Narrow channels here and there block the flow.

We know we must pass beyond our knowing and we fear the shedding.

But we are pulled upward nonetheless through forgotten ghosts and unexpected angels.

Knowing it doesn't make sense to make sense anymore.

The simple brilliance of Buddhist mindfulness led ten years ago to a series of experiences that, quite without warning, took me beyond anything I had ever seen or known.

One quiet evening on the couch, Ondrea and I talking, I excused myself to go to the bathroom. Leaving the bathroom, I was stymied! I did not know which way to turn. I was bewildered and, in reality checking, found I did not even know what day or year it was. At first I thought I might have experienced a slight stroke of some sort. But a feeling of bewildered trust and a sense that this was the next perfect step told me to stay open to unexpected grace.

I did not know who I was or where I was, but I knew everything worth knowing.

Oddly, fear did not arise, but instead an increasing sense of confidence and feeling of being "realer." Less of the all too tight two-dimensional ordinary and more a sense of the bottomless well of Being.

I had the feeling of being found, though I didn't quite know who I was. I was without a boundary by which to be defined. It was perfect.

After a few hours I once again knew date and place. And how much was available when the top of the skull feels like it is about to melt.

The next time this phenomenon occurred was about six months later. As I was drinking a glass of lemonade, all of a sudden the cold delight in my stomach disappeared as the sensations at the top of my head became very intense.

It felt like something was about to break through.

A high-pitched continuum in the ears and in the bones.

Once again, only surrender was enough to stay open to the considerable energy flowing through, which at times felt like pushing 240 volts through a 120-volt carrier.

Though earlier initiations and transitions had raised the stakes, I was still not quite prepared for what was to come.

It was in some ways not unlike the classic mystical experience of waking to look in a mirror to discover that, along with the miraculous, momentary disappearance of your obstructive conditioning, your head seems somehow missing as well. Instead, when I looked in the mirror, the mirror was gone and only the "looking awareness" remained.

A clear light rising from the inner eye, the intense waves of energy rippled across the inside of my head and broke the roof of my skull. (Was this somehow related to the "roof beam" that Buddha said must be broken to be freed of the momentum that in each life rebuilds the body/house of our karma?)

As light merged with light, as space dissolved into space, the energy geysered through time and bone and superstition, through everything known, and expanded ever outward into certain deathlessness.

A very settled sense of being a part of the whole embracing the heart as, deeper yet, microcosm and macrocosm become interchangeable. A galaxy in every tear.

And just before it disappeared over the horizon, the mind asked, "Whatever became of time? It used to be there whether you needed it or not. But now there is only a moment here and there, nothing more or less."

The truth was too big for the cornered mind and pierced the surface of the dream . . . as timelessness condensed into space and time.

Almost a year into this mystery, I mentioned it to a spiritual friend and asked if he thought these rather odd experiences might be of physical origin. He smiled like our old teacher and said, "Sounds like Mother Kundalini to me. And Mother Kundalini will have her way!"

It was an upwelling of the essential energy some refer to as life force, *chi*, or *kundalini* and shamans note as spirit power.

This series of *kundalini* experiences continued for eight years, recurring every six to ten months.

The legacy of such experiences is that we find in the world within gardens and crucifixions, and glances that took twenty years to cross the room. Words not heard until long after those lips had passed their last breath. Roses fragrant for a lifetime. And poems that surprise us in our sleep.

Though this shattering of what limits space has led to some remarkable experiences, it can get rather tricky at times. What at first lasted just a few hours and remained as a period of unusual clarity for a day or two afterward became over time a series of experiences that lasted for days and whose clarity in its wake remained for weeks.

At times I was a bit disoriented and fatigued by their intensity.

The expanding of essential energy intensifies everything, both pleasure and pain.

The attributes and symptoms of *kundalini* include the full range of states of mind as well as many unusual physical phenomena. Hair and nails grow very rapidly. Sometimes people's words and lips seem out of sync. There is a high sensitivity to light. Sometimes there is seen a very fine rain of energy. Occasionally streaks of light seem to extend from living things, trees corona with an aura like smoky gold dust.

Eating only the mildest of foods, yogurt and tofu, no fire. In India the teacher may give students having difficulty with *kundalini* energy meat and sugar to bring them down.

This opening is often preceded by fear, even a turning of the stomach. Sometimes there is a sound like a jet taking off (the dharma lion's roar) or a locomotive approaching that rapidly evolves into a very high frequency pitch.

Moving through level after level of consciousness, passing through all manner of cathedrals and graveyards along the way. The first stages of the opening are reminiscent of the psychedelic experience. A bit of the "retinal circus" as depicted in the *Tibetan Book of the Dead* gives form a run for its money.

And a not altogether pleasant feeling of voltage overload until the top of the head begins to open like a flower unfolding in the sun. Perhaps that is why in some schools of thought this process is called "opening the thousand-petal lotus." The energy thick as molasses slowly spreading out from the center of the crown until the top of the head is completely gone. A sense of presence expanding out through the opening until there is much more of me out and above than down and within. This is not an out-of-the-body experience; this is an other-than-the body occurrence.

In the vastness there is a seeing of oneself in a much greater context. We are at once as infinitesimal as a grain of sand on an endless beach and as boundless as the universe containing every sacred thing.

Everything composed of that which composes consciousness.

The teeth ring with current.

Enormous gratitude and a feeling like having won the lottery.

Irreducible oneness and a slight increase in psychic sensitivity.

When the fear that precedes the opening arises, the heart must insist and be willing to lose it all. We must leave everything at the door. Even our proprietary love of God. Rising up the flume of the spine, leaving Plato's cave behind, merging back into the light.

FORTY

ego death

The day I awoke with no center of gravity, my heart knew it had blown its mind. There was an open cauldera where once my haircut neatly grew.

I seemed a cartoon character of myself dreamed up to keep the mind from being bored.

When in 1975 I went through the dark night of our collective grief while studying with Sujata, it was only the first of that sort of mind-jarring initiation that occurred over the years.

Having been reborn years before out of that dark night that gives rise to such a bright dawn, both of which required substantial re-adjustment, I was deeply inside the Great Question, *Who am I?* being processed by the mystery.

There arose a series of experiences in which no separate self was to be found, which at first left me feeling rather lost and bewildered.

Indeed, a darker night for the soul awaited in what the ego wants to call "ego death." But the ego doesn't really die; it just has a near-death experience. It just stretches the self into the Self, becoming unrecognizable as it expands past previous personal fallacies and long-established false identities.

Ego death is when our idea of who we are, which we fear will be diminished by confronting some deeply self-image-threatening, existence-questioning, rather unpleasant truths, actually breaks its boundaries. We become confused, even frightened, when we cannot identify who is missing in the midst of unending presence.

We presume that an ego death is the end of our hard-won bigness, but actually it is the end of our smallness.

In what is called ego death it should be remembered that the word "ego" simply means "I am," and that it is the sense of "I" that is transformed, not the "am-ness" that is eternal being.

Listening past all the ramblings and rimshots of the hard-postured self, awareness settles into the field of sensation, exploring the sense of presence.

Entering first the sensations that are the basis for the belief we exist, we find a flow of moment-to-moment sensation, but it is noticed that the "I am" is only an afterthought. Not really "the doer," more just another doing.

"*Neti, Neti,*" the aspirant repeats, "Not this, not that," as they dig deeper and wider to find who it is in there, to find something solid enough, permanent enough, to still be real by the end of the sentence. But it all dissolves like flowers in air. The deeper you go the less the question is involved with either the "*who*" or the "*I*" of Who am I? but more a reflection on, and of, endless *am-ness*.

As we explore beyond our accumulated identities, the "*who*" and the "*I*" of the question, being so much heavier than the whole truth, fall back to earth. And only the am-ness remains. Only the unending essence of being, of deathless suchness, to silently answer the question.

There is nothing found small enough to be limited to the mind/body.

In the course of breaking the narrow confines of the self-image, a whole new world becomes available when you find out who you aren't, including your suffering, which wipes out most of your precious/painful identity. This can be a little disconcerting.

Just before my face fell off, I looked back at my life as though it were my own. I was possessed by memory.

But as I passed behind the well-woven tapestry of appearances, history was undone. The knots and snags that hold the illusion in place unraveling.

The suffering defended so long dissolved like the Cheshire smile as a karmic wind caught a loose end and pulled . . .

In transit beyond the known.

These experiences resemble death in that at first they may be met by considerable resistance and fear, but eventually they teach us how to break through to love. After a pound or two of perspiration they lead to considerable healing and insight.

As the series of ego-challenging experiences continued, crossing the no-man's-land beyond the boundaries of the habitual mind, anything resembling a familiar face, particularly my own, seemed a long dark night away. That self-protecting, self-defeating, fear-at-the-edge noticed floating nearby.

A subtle nausea begins to rise in my gut.

The free-floating fear of the unknown, which attempts to placate every anxiety from the will-to-live to sabertooth-behind-the-bush, signals going beyond our edge and entering our great unknown. A letting go of those places of holding past which we seldom venture. Beyond the cage of our safe territory, our limitations, our attachment to old models of who we think we are or should be.

All that ordinarily seems so solid and girds the precious mental construct of the self, no longer able to support its own weight. The illusion as unstable as quicksand, we cross the shifting ground of ordinary mind, as if traversing a haunted cemetery at midnight. Being ever so diligent not to wake the dead.

Opening, as into Big Mind, without clinging to or condemning the moment-to-moment unfolding of rapidly changing states of mind, we begin to notice how mechanically one thought dissolves into the next.

Observing consciousness more as process than content, we continue to cross this no persons' land with mercy and awareness, with gratitude and love for all the wounded and dying identities shed along the way. All the identities that litter the path as this thought or that image, as son, father, man, poet, meditator, seeker, prisoner, teacher, saint, and fool. Passing through the fear that once kept my suffering in place, what had been a fearsome guardian was gradually becoming something of a tour guide. Life accessed at yet another level.

Observing from the still point of the heart everything as just thought. No reality other than thought. Nothing to be feared and no one fearing. Even the thinker just a thought.

After years of being met by a merciful awareness, this fear that heralded greater openings now received with genuine gratitude. With very little inclination to stop the fear or protect the edge, level after level of letting go allowed one imagined boundary after another to fall away.

Just over the ridge above the eyes that separates us from prehistory, unimaginable being expands into inconceivable space.

This boundaryless vista can arouse survival mechanisms that emanate a kind of terror greater than that of dying: the fear of nonexistence. This unfamiliar vastness, offering no milestones or old trailmarkers, can easily disorient small mind into something of a "dark night." A feeling of being lost in edgeless space can occur that leads occasionally to the identity confusion and common grief sometimes confronted in what has been come to be called "spiritual emergencies." This hide-and-seek with the self, this confusion, is most often caused not from just experiencing the unending openness of spiritual emptiness but from, when turning to ourselves for an answer to "Who am I?" we discover only the cold vacuity of our psychological emptiness.

It is here perhaps that we might address the much misunderstood Buddhist concept of "nonself." Indeed, in the face of such terms, much less such experiences as ego death, a student of Buddhism might ask, "How can there be an ego death if, as we are taught, there is no self?"

But of course to say there is no self is absurd and very misleading. The self is a perfect example of what is called a "real illusion." The self is simply an idea of itself. A long-grasped concept that reflects the mind's fears like Narcissus's pond. Of course there is a self; it is a mental construct, a long accumulated fantasy of who we are. To say that this "self"-thought is not founded on anything "real" abiding autonomous at the center would be more accurate. To say there is nothing smaller than our essential enormity that we might even consider calling "I" would be closer to the truth.

When we experience levels of consciousness in which thoughts of self and any other thought carry the same weight—are equally appreciated in an undifferentiated awareness, with no differentiation between the idea of ourselves and the idea of others—a delightfully egolessness ensues.

Which brings us to the realization that if it were true that there was no self, we wouldn't have to work so hard. The ego/self wishes to be present at its own funeral; it's been working on its obituary most of its life. Nothing would make it prouder, identifying itself with such as nonself philosophies, than to be seen as having been uprooted. As the old joke goes, "Look who thinks they're nobody!"

That evening, in meditation, in the absolute silence I could see it hanging there like an old overcoat. It was my personality ego: its likes and dislikes, its inclinations and attitudes, its justifications and imagined personal history.

It was what Joseph Goldstein used to warmly refer to as "the whole catastrophe!" It was "the me" to be put on like a heavy garment. Displacing the sun and stars from my true skin, leaving me cold and in need.

It seemed the dynamics of things (the mystery) had simply dealt me a personality. It wasn't *my* personality; it seemed just to be the one donned to suit the long day.

The personality seemed at the time such an obvious and pathetic joke. Another primitive artifact. A second skin always one step away from the infinite. But then again *only* one step!

But with ego-death experience as with a physical death, it's easier to die than to stay dead, and what do you do with that painful old self-image after a glimpse beyond the kasina and our farthest, most treasured horizon?

After seeing into the nature of thinking and the thinker?

After the origins of consciousness are realized? After form and all that we know and believe appear as but a tiny bubble on the frothy tip of one very small wave amongst innumerable greater waves on a boundless ocean?

And perhaps the best answer to that question of what to do with one's life after one awakens was well offered by one of Kerouac's dharma bums who, when asked what he was going to do with the rest of his life, answered, "Just watch it."

To deconstruct the compulsions of the given personality, to settle back while stepping in, takes strength and courage. To go beyond the familiar and open to the transpersonal, universal miracle of just being is to unlock the personality. Not to cure it, of course, but simply to offer it some care and healing. To loosen some of its bonds and live a bit more lightly, relating to rather than from the chaos-oriented ordinary mind. To allow our intentions a bit more clarity and patience as we take the next step inward toward healing.

Sudden wholehearted comprehension said: *cut out the middle man, the proprietary interpreter of the senses.* Live directly. Truth resides as a dormant grace in the cells like hidden flowers in a rain forest waiting to become cures when at last the illness is acknowledged.

The deepest truth cannot be spoken. The mystery has nothing to press its tongue against; it cannot speak. Only the illusion can be described.

But observing the personality, clearly *I was not that.* But rather the awareness by which it was seen. The luminous space between the atoms and desires that created it.

The personality, as ill-fitting as it seemed, could nonetheless be recognized as a necessary dynamic at this stage of evolution. In the same way that one cannot have a voice without a tone of voice, so we cannot have *being* without a way of being, a personality.

Our personality is the shape of our grief, the manner in which we deal with our pain. A coping mechanism. A driving force from life to life that benefits greatly from the teachings of the heart.

Seen as *the* personality rather than *my* personality, it settles down and stops taking itself so seriously, often experiencing an expanded sense of being. Of the personal uniting with the universal.

Passing through strata after strata of consciousness, there comes a silence so deep that form cannot manifest.

A bliss ensues in which even a single molecule can accommodate the big bang. And I Am That *(Om Tat Sat)* for three billion years rather than become anything less.

Years before I received Terry Southern's note in prison that "poetry was too easy," my resistance to that idea was quite evident.

The poet model may have saved me from drowning, so I was not so quick to put it aside. Actually, at the time it was a skillful deep illusion that kept me upright so I might find the ground beneath my feet and take a further step on the path.

In the adolescence of my spirituality I imagined the highest good would be to become an enlightened poet. Little did I realize that one of the models I would eventually have to break through was the concept of enlightenment. No one gets liberated who still holds to that churchlike dictum. We must first realize that we are a verb, not a noun. That poet is to poetry as religion is to spirit. That one stands small and alone while the other partakes wholly of the enormous universe.

My attempt to defend my identity as poet provided me the opportunity to see the discomfort of attachment to any model at all, even "poet," the best identity I had so far. These signposts pointing toward a distant horizon had suitably confronted me with my own confusion.

As one of my teachers would later point out, "poet" was the lifeline I had used to pull myself from the swamp, but it could very quickly become the hangman's rope to which I was most attached. To paraphrase the teacher's warning, "Don't be a poet. Don't be a saint. Don't be anything small enough to be defined. If you are anything apart from the whole you will suffer!"

If *absolute presence* is being sought, we cannot stop anywhere.

Any identity, good or bad, can be a burden.

FORTY-ONE

discovering our original fire

We have noticed on occasion that some people look with suspicion on mystical experiences. Indeed as Buddhism in America has become, in a very healthy manner for this country, more psychologized, distrust in such metarational experiences has taken some of the miraculous, uncontrollable wonder of the dharma out of the equation.

Ondrea and I have long discussed the possibility that all spirituality, and eventually religion, may have originated many thousands of years ago in deserts, forests, and caves from the inordinate but natural occurrence of spontaneous body-shaking, mind-glistening, spirit-revealing mystical uprisings. Profound releases from within giving rise to such as prophecy and healing powers. It was the discovery of original fire.

A sharp pain flashes across the right side of the head. It says God is coming, sit up straight!

The tectonic plates in the skull are shifting. Lightning in the temporal lobes. Angels, to say the least, and the simple clarity that reveals the floating worlds.

It is like awaking in a dream to find you are not dreaming. Discovering that all along the dreamer was the dream and only this wakefulness is real.

And the body melts from consciousness to consciousness as it dissolves luminous and beyond description.

There are earthquakes in the skull that rattle our silverware and knock all our trophies off their shelves.

They break the roof beam and scatter our belongings, leaving us naked and unidentifiable in the brilliant light.

Those evolutionary insights spread quickly around the fire pit. Insight into the mystery and a sense of the possible and the miraculous followed.

As the mind breaks boundary after boundary, each time the world is born and destroyed, a truer voice is heard. From the shamanic paintings in Lascaux to the bodhisattvas and devas of the Ajanta Caves, from the mystical serpent coiled at the foot of the Bodhi Tree and The Cross, golden possibilities arise.

When thousands of years ago the light spontaneously presented itself under spreading banyan trees or effulgent out of the darkness of the cave, shattering the body, melting the mind, and revealing the spirit, only a few could find the words, could say, *everything is impermanent and full of grace*.

Most have gone mad looking for a solid center, but there is none.
We think of centering as a continual narrowing of focus
until we touch the pearl . . .
but in practice centering is a continual expansion of focus
until we become the ocean.

*The deeper we go, the less definable we become, but the more real
we feel.*
*The deeper we go, the more the luminosity of mind illuminates
our birthright.*
Our center is vast space, boundless awareness.

This emptiness, this vast egoless space at the center, is not nothing,
it is simply no thing, no boundary, no opposite, no exclusion, no inclu-
sion, no birth, no death, no life, no absence of life. Undifferentiated
presence, pure awareness indistinguishable from pure love.

FORTY-TWO

vows taken and returned

Do not take these high-energy experiences, no matter how grateful my hyperbole, as in any way necessary for liberation. I have experienced them for years, and I certainly am not enlightened. Indeed they can even become a distraction if we see them as some sort of personal property.

Many exquisite beings have not had any such showy displays yet have obviously missed nothing, emanating a wisdom and compassion that is a model for many. As both the Gradual and Sudden Schools of Buddhist practice repeatedly remind us, the Gradual School is full of sudden wordless understandings and the Sudden School too seems to take forever. Indeed revelations of truth, gradual or sudden, are only as valuable as our capacity to integrate them into our ordinary life. There is no enlightenment degree or tournament cup; there is just kindness and clarity.

Such experiences as the intermittent *kundalini* upwellings can be misinterpreted by a hungry ego as enlightenment experiences. Which, in a manner of speaking, they are, but not in the way the grasping ghost would like to permanently imprint it on its T-shirt.

Even enlightenment experiences—which of course give rise to enlightened moments and enlightened actions, not enlightened beings—though they may take the roof off, may not completely stabilize the ground on which that now roofless house stands.

Indeed, what most call "enlightenment" does not perfect the personality, only the point of view.

Bottom-dwelling inclinations can appear quite unexpectedly. Karmic bundles, though far too heavy to lift, have been known to float to the surface with sufficient provocation.

We must be aware of the cosmetic quality of spiritual practice. Every time I hear of a person of high reputation "falling," it does not create doubt in me but confidence. It is reassuring to see that a person can be quite extraordinary and still have a lot of work yet to complete.

As one teacher repeatedly reminded us, no matter how far we rise into the mystery, we must keep our feet on the ground.

Though I have had my moments of "god drunkenness," to whose unabashed wholeheartedness I am still somewhat attached, after all is said and done it is the simple clarity of seeing that mindfulness affords that most inspires me. In India the god-drunken need sometimes be directed away from staring too long into the sun.

What is most important is not to lose the present in which presence is to be found, the soul of the mystery that floats in what the early mystics called "the cloud of unknowing."

About three light months after a series of intense upwellings the mystery manifested the next teaching one morning when our old Rottweiler's pained erratic breathing called us out of meditation. It's not like we hadn't been drawn out of meditation dozens of times before by "outside exigencies." Indeed, perhaps a hundred times during the raising of three children. But for some reason, or no reason at all, this day it was all to come together and I received the teaching a bit deeper.

After the pills under his favorite tree watching the birdfeeders, our dear old dog dropped his head. And began the sleep that would gradually loose him from his long-degenerating body.

A good time to lay down his sweet head before the myasthenia gravis completed its neuromuscular degeneration. Breathing with such difficulty, throat collapsing, his jaw locked, back legs dragging, the light dulled in his deep brown eyes. A good day to die. And as we sing, his breathing at last softens after months of unsuccessful medication and increasing weakness.

But a bird song or slight breeze would lift his head for just one more taste of the life he loved so well. Even the cats that he had so often chased sitting just a few feet away.

Until a last warm breeze raised his head for just one last look down the valley across the forest. And with a swoon he laid down his great head and began his last rough snore.

Two crows rising out of the west circled overhead calling RAM RAM RAM, three times around then off to the east.

His crows, his forest, his family all about and so very close.

We buried him under the great lightning-struck ponderosa near the house.

Afterward, watching the sun set, I reflected on how reluctant I had been earlier to transfer my awareness back to the noisy need-filled room. Gradually the selfishness of the pursuit of enlightenment became all too painfully clear to me. I experienced at a level not previously recognized what the enormous generosity of the Bodhisattva Vow might actually be all about.

As the endless heart whispered

"Even though you see there is no such thing as time you have not yet finished the course!

"Even though you see that nothing is real in the way you thought it was, sentient beings still are suffering. With incarnation comes responsibility; beings need each other's help.

"If you forgot everything you knew would you, like he, be able to find your way by the light of your compassion and natural grace?"

How readily, without a mindful thought, I would go to the highest point above sea level, safe above the flood, removed from the common wound and our collective healing. And sometimes miss the mark.

There arose a generosity capable of counterbalancing even the personal confusion that might allow one to pass by suffering without a glance in either direction.

Like that time when the car careened onto the sidewalk on the other side of the street, throwing people through plateglass windows or crushing them against parking meters. And we all ran across the street to help. Kneeling in the glass, tending a badly cut woman, I looked about for someone to aid the young man bleeding next to us. But there were only a few helping the injured. The street was a tableau of people frozen in midaction. Or should I say frozen in inaction. Some had gotten to the curb and stopped. Some had only made it halfway across the street. A few had only gotten one foot off the curb. It wasn't that they didn't want to help, they just couldn't. Frozen in their "safe place," useless.

But for those that made it all the way into the suffering, there was a moment at the edge where only concern for another existed. A moment rich in human interconnectedness. A moment closer to the reason we took birth.

Suzuki Roshi said, "Even if the sun rose in the West the Bodhisattva has but one way." The absolute generosity of the aspirant's vow, of the Bodhisattva's spirit, that cannot, even at the expense of "higher states," leave suffering untended. Committed beyond self-interest to the liberation of all sentient beings. "Unto the last blade of grass so long as space remains."

What we have come to call Infinity is infinitesimal next to the whole truth.

Happiness is a superstition, but joy is our birthright.

Until all things become one thing and that too dissolves into edge-lessness, even words such as these, as the Third Zen Patriarch pointed out, are just "flowers in air."

In the cyclical nature of things, when last year I was asked by an anthologist for a benediction for the millennium celebration, closing my eyes in meditation as I entered time and time again, what arose was very much like the vow of service taken decades before.

There was nothing new to say, the same truths prevail:
Act for the benefit of others
Clear the mind so you can see the way
Remind each other of our true nature
Act with grace for no reason
and stop making excuses
Nothing is random or preset,
so respond from true freedom
Don't let fear or beauty block your way
It takes courage to be moral,
to give up the dissatisfaction
Compassion is fearlessness.

FORTY-THREE

sometimes I

And who, sometimes I, are we after all? When no word or feeling or thought defines the whole? When even the most ambitious concept is too small to describe the most of us? When after a lifetime of learning to breathe, the breath spontaneously returns to the heart?

The breath, begun so many years ago at the center of the chest, which allowed the heart to vent to the surface, connecting with the world, then observed for years at the belly, and for decades at the nostrils, seems to have completed its pilgrimage.

At the center of the chest, where once the grief point pulsed, the breath breathes itself in and out of the touch point of the heart, where mindfulness and devotion converge. Where, to paraphrase one precious teacher, love tells me I am everything. And wisdom tells me I am everything else. "And between these two my life flows."

To approach the heart so very many years before with such uncertainty and return so many years later with such gratitude calls me to bow to the preciousness of the path to liberation.

There is no song more agreeable to the heart than the slow, even breath of a pilgrim learning to bless, and be blessed by, the mystery.

glossary

a collection of conceptual dreams and near definitions

bardo: A term used in the *Tibetan Book of the Dead* especially to define the space between lives; the afterworlds we project and encounter after consciousness leaves one body looking for another. But bardo, when we are fully alive, means much more and much less than that. It also means the space between thoughts and the transformative moment.

breath: Too vast for description.

choiceless awareness: The boundless nonjudgmental openness of mindfulness that allows it unattached access to level after level of consciousness.

dharma: Perhaps the most interesting word I have ever come across. Derived from Sanskrit, to Buddhists first and foremost it means specifically the teachings of the Buddha, as in Buddhadharma. It is also used in other spiritual traditions and generally designates spiritual truth or any such teachings. It also can mean one's duty, one's life path.

Indeed, one of the most engaging definitions of dharma is "mind moment"; the ten thousand dharmas, one might even say "moments of truth," that pass through the mind from instant to instant. Dharma stretches from the smallest particle of consciousness to a state of being too great to measure.

existential angst: The profound sense of human isolation and feelings of anger and anxiety about the condition of uncontrollable impermanence and that nagging sense of incompleteness.

grace: That which takes us closer to our true nature; or, from another point of view, our true nature itself.

heart: A deeper level of consciousness in which the individual may connect with the universal. The small melts into the enormity.

hungry ghost: A Buddhist term for a state of being traditionally represented as a ghostlike figure with a huge belly, a gigantic mouth, a pencil-thin neck, and limbs like sticks. A creature unable to satisfy its gargantuan hungers or quell its enormous desires. The avaricious hungry ghost of unsatiated desire.

Of course the modern hungry ghost has adapted a somewhat different appearance. Nowadays there are ascots, credit cards, and plastic surgery.

interbeing: A term coined by the remarkable Vietnamese Buddhist teacher Thich Nhat Hanh, the organizer of the Buddhist Peace Fellowship for Reconciliation, to indicate the interdependence of all being.

A sense, greater than even empathy, of oneness that leads to the experience of a sharing of consciousness and the life force.

Jesus: "When you say, 'Jesus was waiting for you when you got home late at night from being with a patient in the hospital,' what are you talking about? Do you mean he was corporally present? That you saw him standing there before you?"

"Well, in this case I mean that Jesus comes in the form of a very strong state of mind that opens into a state of being that is crystalline clarity and compassion."

karma: A term from spiritual physics used in Buddhist and Hindu thought to signify the cultivation of inclinations and tendencies from previous thoughts and actions. It is a concept that can be as misleading and even manipulative in those religions as the doctrine of original sin is in Christian belief. In actuality karma simply indicates momentum. Based on the intention behind it, an action is not good or bad, just healing or pain-attached.

Karma is who we are when we let life unconsciously happen to us. Karma is the teaching, when we are paying attention, that by defining blessings and hindrances directs us away from the causes of suffering.

Of karma Buddha said, "This arises, that becomes."

An example of the momentum based on intention that follows the laws of karma is the unfoldings of those two grammar-school friends with whom I walked home.

When last I heard, my sweet, slow, other-minded friend was working quite contentedly close to one of his first loves, at the Motor Vehicle Department.

I encountered Hap twenty-five years after I had last seen him at an editor friend's home in New York City. Following a nervous announcement by my friend that "a big-time dealer friend was coming over and I should be cool, something had gone wrong," in came a very bedraggled Hap. He had just been released from six hours in the trunk of a business associate's car who decided not to kill him after all.

And I marveled once again that somehow between the path too slow and the negligent fast lane the will toward mystery provided the middle way of Buddhism.

koan: A Zen means of peeling back level after level of mind; a little riddle for the frontal lobes that has no logical, only an intuitive suprarational, response.

mantra: A verbal repetition used to powerfully focus the mind. Often a sacred phrase transmitted from teacher to pupil with added emphasis on the lineage of the words handed down over the centuries. Although the only time I met Krishnamurti, his parting statement to me, relating to his feeling that any words will do for a mantra when the heart is in the right place, were, "Coca Cola, Coca Cola!"

mind/body: One day during a particularly well-balanced meditation I got up and for the first time did a perfect headstand.

With the mind and heart well balanced and at peace, it occurred to me that this stillness, this wholehearted balance, must be as present in each cell as it was in each molecule of mind.

When the mind comes into balance, so does the body. Perhaps that's why some say the body is just another level, a grosser stratum, of the vast expanse we so very oversimply call mind: the consciousness that solidifies into matter at one extreme and is boundless suchness at the other (in which there is no "other," but only the One Itself itself).

mindfulness: Attention focused on the moment-to-moment process of the unfolding of consciousness. A penetrating nonjudgmental awareness of physical and mental changes.

ordinary mind: The conditioned cognitive factor residing in the first few layers of consciousness.

presence: The experience of awareness in oneself or another; first noticeable in the field of sensation as the ever vibrating spirit that supports the concept that we exist.

On another level the essence of this presence is the essence of Being. It is recognized as that which does not move during motion, the still point, the only unchanging experience of a lifetime. The underlying hum of essential being, the am-ness to which "I am" refers. Because no beginning of it or end to it can be discerned, some constrain its boundlessness with concepts such as soul or Godhead. And in my writing I too limit its inconceivable vastness by shrinking to it "the Deathless," although it is that and so much more.

right effort: How and where to express right action. An exploration of the possibility of balanced "trying." Doing the right thing for the benefit of everything.

spirit time: We must have spirit time or we will never be able to complete our birth or our death.

How many times a day do we turn toward the mystery?

How many simple prayers while waiting?

How many mindful breaths?

How often converted to compassion is fear and anger?

How often is the song heard singing from ocean to ocean in our body?

How willing are we to go beyond the known, to end the war, to rest in being?

How many times into the heart, breath by breath like a stairway up to the roof of the skull, doors, hatches, skylights opening, decoded from the mind to the heart . . . the mystery breathing forward . . . looking for what is looking . . . and finding what we have always been looking for: the heart to meet our pain and joy with grace and gratitude.

And looking directly into Being know that we are God and that's just the beginning.

thinking: The story line begun by a single thought that attachment invites to continue. That single image unfolding into multiple imagery.

Whether a flight of fancy or linear planning, this process unattended by a deeper awareness keeps us shallow.

thought: A single mental image, perhaps a recollection of one of the senses, arising quite spontaneously in the mind.

underdream: We tend to call the underdream the subconscious, but this is only because we are subattentive.

When one quiets in meditation, thoughts ordinarily too faint to perceive come into focus. Much of what is labeled as "subconscious" is there among the nearly translucent commentary. Beneath the gross is the subtle. Beneath any thought large enough to catch our attention are the subtle contributing factors that forced it to the surface, the tendencies from which it arose. With this subtle seeing we pierce the surface of the underdream.

Beneath our waking dream, if you listen truly, another heartbeat can be discerned.

witness: Not a separate entity within, but that which observes such passing fancies. Awareness itself. Not a "who," but a "what." Not the I of "I am," but the am-ness.

yantra: The visual equivalent of a mantra.